Accounts Receivable
Management
Best Practices

Accounts Receivable Management Best Practices

John G. Salek

WILEY

John Wiley & Sons, Inc.

Published by John Wiley & Sons, Inc., Hoboken, New Jersey.
Published simultaneously in Canada.

For general information on our other products and services, or technical support, please contact our Customer Care Department within the United States at 800-762-2974, outside the United States at 317-572-3993 or fax 317-572-4002.

Wiley also publishes its books in a variety of electronic formats. Some content that appears in print may not be available in electronic books.

For more information about Wiley products, visit our Web site at www.wiley.com.

Library of Congress Cataloging-in-Publication Data:

Salek, John G.
    Accounts receivable management best practices / John G. Salek.
        p. cm.
    Includes index.
    ISBN-10: 0-471-71654-5 (cloth)
    ISBN-13: 978-0-471-71654-9
  1. Accounts receivable.   I. Title.
    HF5681.A3S23 2005
    658.15'224—dc22

                                    2005003023

10 9 8 7 6 5 4 3 2 1

This book is dedicated to the people and institutions who have helped me immeasurably through the years.

My parents, who persevered in their lives through the Great Depression and World War II to provide a wonderful childhood environment for my brothers and I to grow up and be happy in our chosen endeavors.

My brothers, who walked beside me during the early years and who have since prospered in their chosen professions.

Linda, the love of my life and my wife of 27 years, who has been at my side the majority of my adult life, providing support and stability.

Our two children, Michael and Stephanie, who have been an unending source of joy and pride.

The teachers, professors, and coaches at Ramapo High School in Franklin Lakes, New Jersey; The University of Connecticut; and The Amos Tuck School of Business Administration at Dartmouth College; who provided the educational foundation to succeed.

Bob Troisio, my mentor at International Paper Company, who introduced me into the field of receivables management over a quarter of a century ago.

▶ CONTENTS

► PREFACE

In today's global marketplace, competitive pressure and industry practice mandate that products and services be sold on a credit vs. cash-on-delivery basis. This practice often produces a receivables asset that is one of the largest tangible assets on a company's balance sheet. A review of the 2004 Fortune 500 certainly reveals this truth. Receivables ranked among the top three tangible assets for 75% of the top 100 companies. Surprisingly, management of this multi-million (or multi-billion) dollar asset rarely receives much senior management attention, except when a serious problem develops. The custodians of the receivables asset are similar to umpires of a baseball game; they are not noticed unless they do a bad job.

This book discusses the importance of managing accounts receivable, and provides proven principles for achieving benefits such as increased cash flow, higher margins, and a reduction in bad debt loss. The focus is primarily on commercial (business to business) receivables management. It excludes the specifics of managing retail (business to consumer), healthcare provider (third party reimbursement), and intercompany receivables. The principles described apply to all business-to-business commerce, but will often need to be tailored to industry-specific practices.

The Best Practices in this book are real-world, field-tested practices. They were developed, refined, and improved by the author over a 16 year period while working with over 100 companies in a wide range of industries to generate tangible, measurable improvements in the management of customer receivables. Examples drawn from those engagements will be used throughout the book to illustrate real-world problems and solutions that drive measurable results.

This book is designed for all managers who are responsible for managing the receivables asset, either directly, such as directors of customer financial services and credit managers or indirectly, such as controllers, treasurers, and CFOs. Reading this book will enable readers to better understand how to manage this important asset while learning numerous practical techniques that can be implemented immediately to drive improvement.

CHAPTER 1

Introduction

WHY IS RECEIVABLES MANAGEMENT IMPORTANT?

It can be argued that revenue generation is the most critical function of a company. Dot-com companies that created exciting new products but failed to generate significant revenue burned through their cash and ceased operating. Every company expends substantial resources to generate increasing levels of revenue.

However, that revenue must be converted into cash. Cash is the lifeblood of any company. Every dollar of a company's revenue becomes a receivable that must be managed and collected.

Therefore, the staff and processes that manage your receivables asset:

- Manage 100% of your company's revenue.
- Serve as a service touch point for virtually all your customers. (Only Sales and Customer Service speak more with your customers.)
- Can incur or save millions of dollars of bad debt and interest expense.
- Can injure or enhance customer service and satisfaction, leading to increases or decreases in revenue.

If increasing revenue, enhancing customer satisfaction, and reducing expenses are important to you, read on.

The benefits of effectively managing the receivables asset are:

- Increased cash flow
- Higher credit sales and margins
- Reduced bad debt loss
- Lower administrative cost in the entire revenue cycle
- Decreased deductions and concessions losses
- Enhanced customer service
- Decreased administrative burden on sales force

These benefits can easily total millions in profit and tens of millions of cash flow in a year.

IF IT WAS EASY, EVERYONE WOULD DO IT (WELL)

Management of the receivables asset is a demanding task. The vast majority of companies expect that over 99.9% of all billings will be collected. *Collecting ninety five percent of revenue is not good enough.* Companies will tolerate bad debt expense of several tenths of a percent of revenue, but not much more. Which other departments are expected to perform at 99 plus percent effectiveness?

It is generally expected that a high percentage of invoices will be paid on time and over 90% within 30 days of the due date. Management expects that the asset will be managed to promote sales and that all customers will be served promptly, courteously, and professionally. Astoundingly, most firms also expect this all to be accomplished for a cost equal to about *two to three tenths of a percent of revenue. Quite a bargain!*

Management of the receivables asset is a complex task. It addresses the ramifications of practices and processes usually outside the span of control of the responsible manager. It requires balancing of opposing

CASE HISTORY ◀

How Improved Receivables Management Can Revitalize an Organization

A high-technology firm whose products were well regarded by the marketplace was experiencing an especially serious receivables management problem. Bad debt exposure and the investment in receivables were high (days sales outstanding [DSO] was just over 100 days). Millions of dollars in disputed amounts were being conceded annually, not in response to valid customer disputes, but simply as a function of age. In addition, the company's stock price was depressed because of the high DSO. Wall Street analysts interpreted the elevated DSO as an indication that:

- Their new products did not work properly, or
- Products were delivered on a trial basis, were not valid sales, and therefore were not true receivables.

Clearly, this firm was feeling tremendous pain from failure to manage its receivables.

Over an 18-month period, this firm completely redesigned its receivables management process, tools, staff skills, and management culture, implementing most of the principles and techniques described later in this book. The benefits from the company's improvement in its receivables, illustrated in Exhibit 1.1, include:

- A huge increase in the stock price, and
- An increase in cash on hand equivalent to four months of sales.

In addition to the increase in stock price and cash on hand, bad debt and concession expenses decreased by several million dollars annually.

priorities. It is affected by the state of the domestic and global economy, interest rates, foreign exchange rates, banking regulations and practices, business law, and other factors. Excellence in receivables management is a combination of art as well as science; it involves business process, technology tools, staff skills, motivation, company culture, changing behavior of both customers and coworkers, the right organization structure and metrics, incentives, and flexibility to deal with changing external influences.

Exhibit 1.1 Benefits of Improved Receivables Management

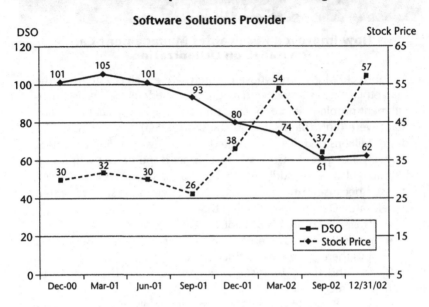

Software Solutions Provider

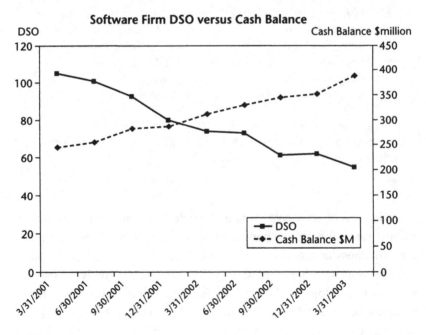

Software Firm DSO versus Cash Balance

Exhibit 1.2 illustrates the determinants or drivers of receivables management. Most of them are outside the direct control of the manager with responsibility for receivables.

INFLUENCES OUTSIDE THE CONTROL OF THE RESPONSIBLE MANAGER

The receivables asset is sometimes called the garbage can of the company. This is because the receivables asset reflects the quality of the entire revenue cycle operation. If an error is made in taking an order, fulfilling it, invoicing it, applying the customer payment, or if the customer is dissatisfied with the product or service, it will manifest itself as a past due or short payment in the receivables ledger. The quality of the receivables asset is an excellent barometer of customer service. It is feedback the customer willingly and quickly gives. It is tempting to call it a free quality control measurement system, except it is not free. The firm does not have to pay customers for the feedback, but it does incur costs in remediating the problems.

Exhibit 1.2   Drivers of Improved Receivables Management

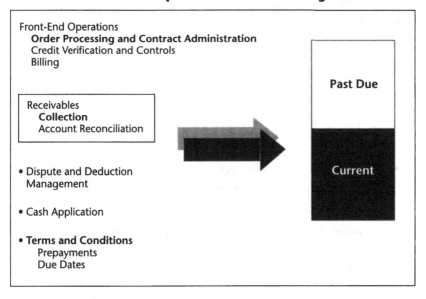

In most companies the sales strategy and/or the front-end operations (i.e., order processing and fulfillment, etc.) are outside the direct management control of the person responsible for receivables management results. In such cases, the manager is measured on the results of a process that he or she does not fully control. In response to this, enlightened companies will place the entire revenue cycle (order to cash cycle) under the control of a single executive, as a "process owner." This arrangement has numerous advantages, the primary one being the matching of authority with responsibility. Even then the executive does not have total control over all the determinants, specifically the sales strategy and the "need to make the numbers" at the end of a month or quarter.

CONFLICTING PRIORITIES

Excellence in receivables management requires trade-offs between conflicting goals. The trade-offs are best balanced in accordance with the company's overriding strategic objectives. To optimize the trade-off, the relative ranking of these strategic objectives must be understood:

- Sales growth
- Profitability
- Cash generation
- Market share
- Risk tolerance

The conflicting objectives are to:

- Loosen credit acceptance criteria and controls to boost sales versus tightening credit controls to minimize the investment in receivables and the exposure to bad debt loss
- Achieve strong receivables management results and provide excellent financial service to your customers versus minimizing the cost of the function

The Best Practices described in this book, when tailored to a company's strategic objectives, culture, and industry, will enable excellence in receivables management in all of its dimensions. This excellence will deliver the profit and cash benefits available to your company.[1]

NOTE

1. *Fortune*, Special Issue, vol. 149, no. 7 (April 5, 2004), pp. F1–F20.

CHAPTER 2

Receivables Antecedents

Receivables antecedents are defined as all the up-front operations required to create a receivable. They include:

- Quotation
- Contract and pricing administration
- Order processing
- Credit control
- Invoicing

This chapter addresses these receivables antecedent functions only as they affect receivables management. Naturally, there is a great deal more information and detail about these functions, but we will limit the discussion as noted.

The antecedents are absolutely critical to the management of the receivables asset. They directly impact the quality and collectability of the asset and are the key driver of the cost to manage a company's revenue stream. A simple formula to illustrate this point is:

High customer satisfaction + Accurate invoice =
Excellent receivables results

This formula holds true even if the core receivables management functions (i.e., credit control and collections) are lacking. Excellent order fulfillment drives high customer satisfaction. In combination with accurate invoicing, the cost of delinquency, concessions, and management of the receivables asset can be dramatically reduced. When competent credit control and collections are added, the total receivables management benefits are maximized.

QUOTATION

Overview

Quotation is the process of extending a formal offer for a product or service to a prospective or existing customer. A clear, complete quotation lays the foundation for excellent fulfillment of a customer order and accurate invoicing.

The two key attributes of a quotation that promote excellent receivables results are:

1. **Feasibility/deliverability of offering.** Do not quote something you cannot deliver. The product or service quoted must be able to be delivered by your firm and perform as sold. If not, the customer will be dissatisfied with the product/service and withhold payment of your invoice

2. **Clear commercial terms and conditions agreed by both parties.** The six elements of a quotation that affect receivables results are:

    1. The unit and total price (clearly stated including all discounts)

    2. Applicable sales or use tax

    3. Freight/delivery (actual versus allowance, who pays it)

    4. Payment terms (when is payment due?)

    5. The timing of issuing the invoice (upon shipment, at the start or completion of a project, on reaching a milestone)

    6. Description of product or service offered (product number, layman's description, proper or trademarked product name).

► **CASE HISTORY** ◄

Make Sure Receivables Management Is the Problem

A European supplier of turnkey computer systems that included hardware, software, and training was experiencing poor cash flow and seriously delinquent receivables. After speaking with collections, customer service staff, and customers, it was apparent that many of the systems were not working as promised. This company did not have poor receivables management processes or practices; it had a product that did not work. Improvement in receivables results could not be achieved without first improving product performance.

► **CASE HISTORY** ◄

Improved Product Performance Leads to Improved DSO

A New England manufacturer of big-ticket production equipment rushed a new product into the marketplace before it was completely debugged. Performance problems developed, customers withheld payments, and DSO approached the 200 level. The manufacturer devised a solution and methodically retrofitted the installed base of the new product. Customers were pleased but insisted on running the "fixed" equipment for 30 days before accepting and paying for it. The retrofit program required six months to complete, but it was successful. The firm's DSO dropped as much as 10 to 20 days per month once the retrofit program progressed, returning to normal levels after approximately eight months. No improvement in receivables management practices was made; the improvement resulted entirely from improvement in product performance.

Best Practices

- Limit quotations to offerings in the approved sales catalog or other official product listing.

- Utilize an automatic "product configurator" tool. Doing this prevents offering a combination of products, options, and/or accessories that are not compatible. An example of incompatibility would be to offer a printer wired for European voltage with a desktop computer wired for U.S. voltage.

- Secure approval and sign-off from engineering and manufacturing for custom products, or from the executive responsible for delivering the service (e.g., project manager for professional services).

- Ensure all quotations clearly state the commercial specifications of the deal. Of course, a customer purchase order may not agree with your quotation. The resolution of this discrepancy will be covered in the "Order Processing" section.

Key Points

- Do not quote and sell products and services you cannot deliver if you want excellent receivables management results.

- The quotation is the first step in fulfilling the customer order exactly and in issuing an accurate invoice. If the quotation is sloppy, payment delays will result.

- An important internal control required to comply with Sarbanes-Oxley and that should be tested by both internal and external auditors is the level of control over:

  - Offering (quoting) products or services the firm cannot deliver

  - Offering unauthorized prices, freight, and/or payment terms

CONTRACT ADMINISTRATION

Overview

From a receivables management perspective, contract administration is all about charging the correct price on the invoice. Price discrepancies are the leading cause of disputed invoices, which result in delayed payments, short payments, and substantial rework. The concept is simple; in practice it is much more complex and difficult.

Contracts are used for larger customers who will receive frequent shipments of products and/or delivery of services over a period of time and are looking to ensure supply and receive the lowest price. Infrequent customers are usually served via individual orders covered by their written, electronic, or verbal purchase order. Contracts govern the commercial terms and conditions of the orders (or releases against the contract) that are received during the time period in which the contract is in effect. As we said in the "Quotation" section, it is vital that the contract clearly define the agreed commercial terms and conditions concerning:

- Price
- Sales and use tax when applicable
- Freight/delivery charges
- Payment terms
- Invoice timing
- Clear description and specification of product and/or services to be delivered

In addition, the time period covered by the contract must be specified.

Best Practices

- The commercial terms and conditions in a contract must not only be clear but *agreed* to by both buyer and seller. Otherwise, invoices will be disputed. A contract signed by both parties is proof of agreement. We have seen many unexecuted contracts being utilized to govern a commercial relationship with a customer. This practice is risky when a dispute is escalated to senior management or to external mediators, arbitrators, or in a court of law. *Get the contract signed*. Ensure the signatory is properly authorized to do so. If in doubt whether a person is authorized, secure a resolution from the board of directors attesting to such authority.

> ► **CASE HISTORY** ◄

Delays on Contract Renewals Cause Receivables Headache

A capital equipment manufacturer had a thriving maintenance business. The majority of its customers were under service contracts that provided preventive maintenance at regular intervals and emergency service as needed. The pricing for a service contract was a fixed annual fee based on hourly rates much lower than the non-contract (time and material) rates. The duration of the contract was generally one year; to continue the service contract, it had to be renewed each year.

Inevitably, contracts would expire, and while customers expressed their intent to renew them, numerous contract renewals were not executed prior to the expiration of the current contracts. What happened?

Emergency service was provided many customers in the period between expiration of the former service contract and renewal of the new one. The customers were billed at the higher time and material rates since technically they were not "contract" customers. The customers did not pay the invoices. They considered themselves contract customers on the verge of renewing retroactive to the expiration date of the former contract. Cash flow decreased, and DSO and past due receivables skyrocketed. When the renewals were finally secured, all of the prior time and material invoices were credited, and new invoices were generated for the service contracts. The rework penalty in terms of staff time and expense was huge. Delinquency costs were significant, and the customers were annoyed with the whole process.

A discrepancy in a single factor (effective date of the contract) was enough to cause huge problems for this capital equipment manufacturer.

- Ensure the contract is in force. The absolute Best Practice is to have an "evergreen" or automatic renewal/extension clause in the contract, which keeps the contract in force until either party formally cancels it.

- The timely renewal of contracts is a universal challenge. The Best Practice is to:

  - Use a system tool (contract administration software application) to track all contracts and their start and expiration dates. The tool should proactively notify those responsible for renewals when a contract is approaching its expiration date.

  - Start the renewal process 90 to 120 days prior to contract expiration, with early and frequent customer contact.

  - Establish a clear policy governing transactions with customers whose contracts have expired. The policy should specify the pricing of such transactions (e.g., should a non-contract price be charged, or should the contract price be used for a grace period?). Customers should be notified of this policy when contacted to renew their contract.

  - Employ a clear escalation procedure involving senior management for contracts fast approaching the expiration date. The procedure should involve sales management to pursue the renewal revenue, but also clearly stipulate the conditions of selling to the customer beyond the expiration date (i.e., prices, terms, etc).

  - In addition to being in force, the commercial terms and conditions have to be kept up to date. Many contracts have provisions for changing prices during the term of the contract. Prices of manufactured goods such as paper and petrochemicals are tied to the commodity market price of key raw materials. Prices of distributed products are often tied to the acquisition cost of the distributor.

- Manage the work flow and backlogs to ensure the contract system is current and accurate. The major problem we have seen over the years is a backlog of new or renewed contracts awaiting input into a company's contract system. This is especially true when a large portion of the contracts expire on the same date (most commonly, December 31). This workload peak can be mitigated by staggering contract expiration dates more evenly throughout the year.

- A second frequent problem is a backlog in inputting price changes into the contract system.

- For both of these backlog problems, our recommendation (in addition to staggering expiration dates) is to allocate more resources to keep the backlogs to a one- to two-day lag. Remember, every invoice that is generated off an incorrect or expired contract will likely be disputed and result in decreased cash flow, rework, and diminished customer satisfaction. The cost of delay is huge and, in most cases, will exceed the cost of a little temporary help.

Key Points

The three key points for excellent contract administration are simple to understand but not easy to accomplish. They are:

1. Ensure all contracts are current (in force).

2. Ensure the price matrices and customer master file data (ship- and bill-to addresses, payment terms, etc.) derived from the contracts are updated and current.

3. Grant access to contract information as widely as possible to individuals performing the collection and dispute resolution functions.

PRICING ADMINISTRATION

Overview

Price discrepancies are the leading cause of invoice disputes. This is not surprising when you think of all the pricing incentives and promotions offered to give a company a competitive advantage and/or to affect customer buying behavior. Examples of pricing mechanisms designed to alter buying behavior are:

- Shifting orders from a busy season of peak demand to a slow season

- Increasing individual order or shipment size

- Increasing total volume purchased within a specified time period and so on.

Many of these pricing incentives overlap and can be quite complex, causing confusion among the supplier's pricing and billing staff and the customer's accounts payables and procurement staff. System tools may not be able to accommodate complicated pricing schemes and accurately price invoices. Unfortunately, the results can be very damaging.

Best Practices

Pricing accuracy is possibly the most important determinant of receivables management success. It is a science in and of itself. However, here are seven fundamental practices that promote pricing and invoicing accuracy:

1. Keep your pricing scheme as simple as it can be. This may not be possible if your competition offers complex pricing incentives.

> ► **CASE HISTORY** ◄
>
> **Complex Pricing Structure Complicates Receivables Management**
>
> A large distributor sold over 50,000 different products whose prices changed sporadically during the year. It maintained individual cost-plus pricing schedules with over 6,000 customers. Each time a manufacturer changed a price on a product, it potentially required a price change in 6,000 customer price schedules. This constituted one of the most difficult price administration challenges we have ever seen. While this customer achieved a high degree of accuracy, it still grappled with a substantial volume of price discrepancies, which impacted invoicing accuracy and receivables management results.

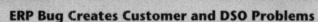

CASE HISTORY

ERP Bug Creates Customer and DSO Problems

A supplier of medical devices to hospitals implemented a new enterprise resource planning (ERP) system. Unfortunately, flaws in the pricing application caused it to default to list price intermittently, thereby generating hundreds of incorrect invoices. Customers refused to pay them, frequently demanding corrected invoices. DSO increased by almost 50%. Delinquency deteriorated so much that the customer's borrowing capacity under its receivable securitization facility was severely restricted. It required thousands of hours of work over a 10-month period to recover from this pricing problem.

2. Ensure all products and services offered have a discrete product (aka, stock keeping unit [SKU]) number, and a price assigned to it in the pricing matrix or master.

3. As stated in the "Quotation" and "Contract Administration" sections, ensure the multiple elements of the price are clearly articulated to both the customer and your internal staff. Six elements of the price are:

    1. List or base price for the SKU

    2. Applicable discounts

    3. Freight terms

    4. Payment terms (including prompt payment discounts) and billing timing

    5. Applicable sales and/or use tax

    6. Late payment fees (finance charges)

4. Ensure all elements of the pricing master and individual customer price schedule are up to date and in force (i.e., not expired).

5. Ensure promotional pricing is adequately controlled; that is, all promotions are authorized and communicated internally and

externally prior to effective date. Utilize off-invoice pricing where possible, so the net price to the customer is clearly stated on the invoice.

6. Ensure all price changes are communicated well in advance of the effective date and that all contracts and price schedules are similarly updated.

7. Utilize a sound dispute management process for pricing and other disputes. For most companies, pricing schemes are complex, and it is inevitable that customers will dispute prices that are indeed correct. A dispute management process will:

► **CASE HISTORY** ◄

Quick Fix Is Costly

A tier 1 supplier of automotive components to the Big Three U.S. automobile manufacturers announced a price increase for its products. After much negotiation, the three customers acquiesced to the price increase. One of the three, however, negotiated a very complex pricing scheme to implement the price increase. It was so complex, its accounts payable system could not automatically process vendor invoices submitted with the new pricing. Programming changes were required to enable such invoices to be automatically processed, and those changes could not be completed for four months. Rather than manually process the huge volume of invoices, the customer insisted on automatically short paying half the invoices and overpaying the other half. The intended effect was to pay the correct amount in the aggregate. A monthly reconciliation and true-up protocol was instituted to verify the correct amounts were being paid. This true-up was spreadsheet and manually intensive, and consumed large amounts of accounting and finance staff time at great expense for both parties. The cause of the added expense was pricing discrepancies.

Once the correct prices were loaded into both the seller's and buyer's systems, and the programming changes were made to the customer's payables application, the invoices were paid promptly and cost effectively. The supplier's receivables results improved, and its costs returned to normal.

- Enable pricing errors to be investigated and resolved quickly so the disputed invoice can be corrected and paid quickly with minimal rework and so that the receivables ledger and financial statements are accurate. Accurate financial statements are the overriding objective of Sarbanes-Oxley legislation. Unresolved pricing errors left open in the receivables ledger are an overstatement of revenue and assets.

- Enable accumulation of dispute causality data that is essential to a continuous improvement effort to increase order fulfillment and invoicing quality.

Key Points

In our experience with over 100 companies in a wide range of industries, business models, and technological sophistication:

- Disputed invoices comprised 50 to 80% of the invoices past due more than a few days.

- Pricing discrepancies were the leading cause of disputed invoices, ranging from 30 to 70% of all disputes.

Clearly, to improve receivables management results, a company must do two things:

1. Price its invoices accurately.

2. Resolve pricing disputes quickly and efficiently.

Also, the controls over pricing will receive substantial scrutiny during audits and Sarbanes-Oxley testing to ensure that only properly authorized prices are offered to customers and that revenue is accurately stated.

CREDIT CONTROLS

Overview

The objective of credit controls is to manage the risk inherent in the extension of credit to promote sales. This risk is known as credit risk, and is the same risk incurred by lenders of money, such as banks. A company that sells only on cash-in-advance or cash-on-delivery terms and requires a secure form of payment has no credit risk. However, unless

▶ **CASE HISTORY** ◀

Breaking the Mold

A manufacturer of capital equipment was the first in its industry to introduce a new generation of diagnostic technology. The equipment was selling fast, and the company wanted to exploit this technological advantage before the competition matched it with similar products. In addition to a strategic goal of maximizing sales in the first years after introduction, other critical factors in managing credit risk were:

- The equipment had a high profit margin (over 70%).
- The company required a 30% down payment with order, which reduced the risk of loss.
- The equipment could be repossessed, refurbished, and resold if necessary, further mitigating the risk of loss.

The company's approach to the credit risk decision was to impose no up-front credit vetting or controls. It sold to whomever placed an order with the down payment. The rationale was:

- The down payment was evidence of a significant level of financial resource.
- The ability to repossess in conjunction with the down payment mitigated risk.
- The profit margin was sufficient to cover bad debt loss over a period of several years and still generate a satisfactory return.
- It was consistent with the strategic goal.

Such a decision was unusual and bold (and not generally recommended). An analysis after the first three years of the program revealed that the number of risky customers who paid in full far exceeded those who failed to pay. The overall profitability of the program surpassed targets. Clearly, tight credit controls would have prevented sales whose profit would have exceeded the bad debt loss incurred, resulting in a lower overall profit. This is an excellent example of a company that evaluated the risk of sales to risky customers versus the profit to be gained and arrived at an unorthodox decision that was right for it.

that company has a product or service that no one else offers, its sales will be much lower employing those terms of sale. The global marketplace runs on credit. Goods and services are routinely delivered with the expectation that payment will be made according to the agreed payment terms.

Credit risk has two dimensions. The first is the risk that payment will never be made. This loss is known as bad debt. The second risk is that payment will be made late; that is, beyond agreed payment terms. This loss is known as delinquency. It is considered a loss on the basis that a company will have to borrow money and pay interest to replace the funds not received on time. Naturally, bad debt loss is the more devastating of the two losses and the risk that receives the most management attention. The high-profile bankruptcies of the past several years (Enron, WorldCom, Kmart, Fleming, etc.) have driven this reality

► CASE HISTORY ◄

Reactive Policy Proves Costly

A multi-billion-dollar (annual sales) provider of recurring professional services to the Fortune 1000 had no proactive credit controls. Its rationale was that it sold to a blue-chip customer base and that if receivables became seriously past due, it would suspend service until the receivables were paid. Unfortunately, this passive, reactive management of credit risk led to substantial bad debt and delinquency losses. The fact that a customer is large and listed among the largest companies in the world does not vouch for its creditworthiness. This professional services provider fell victim to most of the high-profile bankruptcies mentioned above. In practice, the company was slow to recognize serious delinquencies. Suspension of service rarely resulted in significant payments from the customer to bring the account to a current basis. Instead, it was a validation that the customer was in dire financial condition, and bad debt loss usually followed.

This company's evaluation of the risk/reward trade-off was flawed as it underestimated the credit risk of "large" companies. As a result, its losses over a period of years were millions of dollars, particularly in the years 2001 through 2003.

home to thousands of suppliers. It is a constant threat. During the years 2000 through 2003, between 35,000 and 40,000 companies filed bankruptcy each year.[1]

The critical task to managing credit risk is to balance the need for credit sales, and the profit earned on those sales, against the perceived risk of extending credit to a customer. There is no easy answer or magic formula for balancing these factors. The proper balance varies by individual company and is based on a firm's profit margins, strategic goals, and whether a product can be repossessed and resold. There are many techniques and tools to investigate, evaluate, and monitor credit risk; however, balancing that risk against the other company priorities is unique to each firm, requires judgment, and is never easy.

Best Practices

The Best Practices address managing credit risk for both domestic and foreign customers. They will discuss establishing and maintaining credit limits, ongoing controls, credit insurance, and other useful tips for managing credit risk.

Credit Limits

Credit limits quantify the dollar amount of risk a company is willing to bear with an individual customer. It is analogous to the size of a loan or line of credit a bank would extend to one of its customers. In principle, it is a "line in the sand" beyond which the risk is intolerable.

Establishing Credit Limits for New Customers

A credit investigation is necessary to establish a credit limit for a new customer. Best Practices for establishing credit limits for new customers are:

- Start with a credit application from the customer to your company requesting a credit account. The application should include:
  - Customer's legal name, type of entity, tax I.D. number,

contact information, trade and bank references, estimated sales volume.

- Legal language defining your company's credit policy and the terms of granting credit, rights to revoke, late payment fees, etc.

- A signature from the customer formally signifying acceptance of your credit terms.

- Investigate the applicant's credit. If it is publicly held, research its financials on EDGAR, the applicant's Web site, or other service. In many cases, the investigation will end here, as the financials will provide sufficient information.

- If additional information is needed, secure payment, default, litigation, Uniform Commercial Code (UCC) filing, lien, and related information from a commercial credit information provider such as Dun & Bradstreet, Experian, and so on. The industry chapter of the National Association of Credit Managers (NACM) also provides reliable payment history information. Online, electronic (versus hard copy) receipt of this data is Best Practice.

- If you are unable to establish a credit limit with the above sources of information, proceed to check the trade and bank references. This is the reason these references are requested on the credit application. In many cases, you will not need to research these sources, but it is important to have them available when needed. Best Practice dictates that the credit investigation proceed only as far as needed to determine a credit limit. It is inefficient to investigate all information sources if a decision can be reached with one or two sources.

- Evaluate the information and assign a credit limit and a date the limit expires or is to be reevaluated. Best Practice evaluation uses a quantitative credit scoring or risk rating model. The credit score translates into a predetermined range of credit limits. The model can be an in-house model or a model offered by a credit information service. Best Practice credit scoring utilizes automated input of credit information and automated scoring with a calculated credit limit. There is always an option to modify an automatically calculated credit limit with human judgment The credit scoring/evaluation to establish a credit limit should weigh these factors:

- Financial strength (financial ratio analysis).

- Exposure calculated by the sum of estimated monthly sales and customized inventory to be held for the customer, multiplied by the payment terms. The exposure to any related parties (e.g., corporate parent/child relationships) must be added to aggregate total exposure to an entity.

- Payment history with other suppliers as reported by credit reporting service.

- Presence or absence of litigation, referrals to collection agencies, liens, UCC filings, judgments, and so forth.

- Profitability of sales to customer.

- If the credit limit established is inadequate to support the customer's expected trading volumes, the risk of a higher limit can be mitigated by:

  - Deposits, "down payments," or advance payments.

  - Security devices such as letters of credit, guarantees, and/or Uniform Commercial Code (UCC) filings.

  - Shorter payment terms.

The intent of Best Practice credit controls is to find a way to sell to the customer under some sort of credit arrangement. While it may not be prudent to grant the full level of credit desired by the customer (and your sales department), some combination of credit and security can usually be found to enable the deal.

Building a Specific Reserve for High-Risk Customers

Another Best Practice to enable credit sales is special provisioning of the reserve for bad debt for individual high-risk customers. If management still wants to sell on credit beyond the limits the credit investigation indicates is prudent, an innovative technique is to provision the bad debt reserve for a specific customer (or category of customer) at higher rates until the reserve is adequate to cover the risk of the exposure of that customer. Thus, the sale is made, but the added risk is recognized, and over time, the reserve is built up to cover any bad debt loss incurred from the customer(s).

For example, management wants to sell $100,000 per month to a very high-risk customer (i.e., a debtor in possession) on net 30-day payment terms. A credit investigation judges a $30,000 credit limit to be prudent. To enable this trading and cover the risk, all sales to this individual customer would be accompanied by an additional provision to the bad debt reserve of 25% of sales. Over a period of four months, assuming no bad debt loss and the customer paying promptly, thereby maintaining its receivable at $100,000, a specific reserve would exist sufficient to totally cover the $100,000 exposure to bad debt loss. At that point, the specific provisioning would be tailored to maintain the reserve at the same level as the receivable. The company will have gained the profit from the additional sales yet still have recognized the risk of a potential bad debt loss.

Once the credit limit has been established, it should be communicated in writing to the customer with an explanation of how it will be administered (i.e., enforced). This notification is a customer service opportunity, so Best Practice is to send a "Welcome" letter to the customer, welcoming it to your family of customers and explaining how the credit limit works. Include the name(s) of the contacts in the credit department. Sales should be copied on this letter.

After the credit limit has been established, very high limits (the amount will vary by company) should be reviewed and authorized (via signature) by senior finance and executive management to signify their authorization of the credit exposure.

The credit investigation for new customers is an excellent opportunity to exercise control over nonstandard payment terms. All payment terms requested by new customers that are not in the standard offering must be authorized by senior finance and executive management. Best Practice prescribes that credit management forward these to the designated managers for approval with a summary of the financial impact of the nonstandard terms expressed in:

- The cost of financing the receivables for the extended period of time
- The incremental exposure to bad debt loss and the additional expense for the provision for bad debt loss
- The cost of prompt payment discounts
- The profitability of the sales to the customer

When the credit limit for the new customer has been completely approved, authorization to sell the customer on credit terms should be established by creating a customer master file for that customer. Control over creation and update of the customer master file is a key internal control that is the subject of internal and external audit scrutiny. Best Practice prescribes the credit department forwarding authorization to create a customer master file to the controlling department (often the customer service department). The authorization includes the customer's legal name, billing address, payment terms, and credit limit.

Finalize the establishment of a credit limit for a new customer by aggregating all information and source materials in an individual file for each customer. Best Practice is for the file to be electronic, utilizing electronic images of documents where document files are not feasible. A file of hard copy documents is the next best option.

Updating Existing Credit Limits

The financial strength and creditworthiness of companies can change rapidly. For example, information technology services companies that helped their customers prepare for Y2K were fabulously successful in the late 1990s. Yet many of these same companies experienced financial difficulty in 2000 and 2001, with some filing for bankruptcy protection. If you established a credit limit based on 1999 financials for these firms, and did not update it, you incurred serious exposure to bad debt loss.

In many respects, updating a credit limit involves repeating the steps taken in establishing the initial credit limit. However, there are two significant differences:

1. You have the customer's historical payment performance for your invoices. This may be the most reliable and valuable data you have, particularly the trend in that payment performance.

2. You may have better access to the customer's financial statements (if privately held) and better insight into its operations and financial strength. For example, if the volume of orders to you is rising, you can discuss with the customer how its business is progressing, new customers, sources of capital, and so on. As a supplier extending credit and bearing risk, you have a legitimate interest in this proprietary information.

Access to this information will, in many cases, reduce the depth of the credit investigation. If a customer has an on-time payment history with you and its financial statements and/or credit reports are good, then the credit limit can be confidently updated with no further research. The credit scoring model should have the capability to factor in your payment experience with a customer. With a few of the key inputs mentioned above, it should produce a credit score to enable updating of the limit.

Other elements of Best Practice are:

- The timing of the update is a function of the credit limit expiration date assigned when the account was initially established. Customers with excellent financial strength should be assigned a longer expiration date than high-risk customers, whose condition you should monitor more frequently and closely. Remember, cost efficiency is a constant requirement of the receivables management function.

- The system tool should automatically highlight accounts whose credit limits are about to expire in the next 60 days. This allows plenty of time for the credit investigation to be conducted and for the credit limit to be updated with the same or changed credit limit and a new expiration date.

- Updates should also be triggered by adverse events such as:
  - Deterioration in payment performance. This is critically

important information. No system of credit controls can be totally effective without a comprehensive, excellent collection process. Collection is the "eyes and ears" of the credit function.

- A "bounced" check or draft or other electronic payment.
- Business setbacks reported in the press or by a sales rep or other party.
- Alerts from commercial credit information services. Several firms offer a special monitoring service of designated accounts to inform you of adverse events, such as the account being placed for collection, having a judgment or lien, and so on.
- The same approval/authorization hierarchy for initial credit limits should apply to updates.

Credit Control over Ongoing Business

The speed and volume of business today combined with lean staffs makes it easy for credit controls to be evaded or ineffectively applied. To counteract this pressure, two principles must be followed:

1. Some controls should be absolute and enforced by the system.
2. Controls requiring manual involvement should be periodically evaluated to ensure the staff time they consume is worth the benefits they generate.

Examples of absolute controls are:

- A customer number cannot be assigned without a credit limit assigned by an authorized person.
- Products and services cannot be delivered or billed to a customer without a customer number.
- Access to the customer master file, which contains the credit limit and customer number, must be restricted to a few authorized individuals.

- Payment terms for a customer cannot be changed except by an authorized person.

The most important control in the category of manual involvement is the limitation of risk exposure to customers who are over their credit limit and/or delinquent. Best Practice is for the system to prohibit entry of an order and release of shipment of product/delivery of service to a customer who violates the over limit or delinquency tolerances. This control should be a "hard" control, meaning it is impossible to enter an order or dispatch an order for delivery for a customer in violation of the tolerances. A "warning" list of customers in violation that does not prohibit delivery to such customers will be ineffective. Only when the "hard" hold is relieved by an authorized individual, can the order or delivery be processed.

This control should be activated by *either* of the two conditions: over credit limit or delinquency. In the interest of efficiency and speed, tolerances should be established for violation; for example, only customers 5% or more over limit qualify for the "hard" hold. Similarly, the delinquency condition should have flexibility for the amount past due (perhaps > $1,000) and the number of days past due (perhaps 15 to 30). Otherwise, if the tolerances are too tight, the individuals who deal with the holds will be inundated with nuisance cases that are a few dollars or relatively few days in violation. Such nuisance cases consume time and are quickly released anyway. In reality, are you really going to hold an order and contact a customer over a small amount of money that is five days past due? The customer will plead mail delays and be offended, and you will have wasted a lot of time. Inevitably, there will be a select group of customers you want to monitor very closely and keep a tight rein on, but the entire hold mechanism should not be designed for the few.

The Best Practice computation of a customer's receivables to trigger a hold is quite sophisticated. It should exclude three things:

1. Disputed invoices
2. Late payment fees
3. Unearned prompt payment discounts

Items 2 and 3 may be included, but only if your firm historically collects 90% or more of them. Otherwise, you will just introduce "noise" into the system.

Computation to trigger a hold should include:

- Open receivables
- Pending orders
- Customized inventory that cannot be easily resold

Note: The exposure to affiliated customers who are part of the same corporate entity must also be tabulated by the system. This is often called "parent/child" linkage. It enables you to monitor total exposure to a corporate entity. Without this parent/child linkage and tabulation, a company's exposure to a customer with many divisions and subsidiaries will be invisible and uncontrolled.

The credit hold should be processed in three steps:

1. The responsible credit representative reviews the status of the account and total exposure, then formulates the conditions the customer must meet to allow release of the order.

2. The credit representative then contacts the customer and informs it of the situation and of the payments it is required to make to release the hold. Communication of the credit hold to

---

► **CASE HISTORY** ◄

Not Keeping Tabs Company-Wide

A multibillion dollar (annual sales) Fortune 100 company had several divisions that sold to Kmart. They were unable to monitor their total exposure to this customer. When Kmart filed Chapter 11 bankruptcy, not only did they incur millions of dollars in losses, but it took three days to tabulate their total, corporate-wide exposure to Kmart. This is a clear example of lack of control and of getting "blindsided" by bad news.

the customer should always be via a telephone call as soon as possible, not by letter or e-mail.

3. When the payments are made (or in some cases promises to pay), the authorized credit representative releases the hard hold in the system. Only authorized individuals should have access to releasing a hold.

The hold stays in place until it is manually released by an authorized individual. This maintains the highest practical level of control over exposure.

A simple analysis can ensure this control is cost effective. Track the number of orders that are held for a period of time. Calculate:

- The percent of total orders held
- The time spent on releasing the orders (obtain estimates from the staff)
- The percent of held orders released without customer contact (solicit this number from the staff)

If the percent of time dealing with held orders is over a third of total department time, and if more than 10% of held orders are released without customer contact, the criteria for holding an order may be too tight. Interview your staff to get a feel for the time efficiency of the process. In some cases, you may be dealing with an undercapitalized customer base that requires a high volume of held orders to effectively control and manage the asset. In such a case, devoting a third of staff time to credit hold releases may be efficient. However, held orders may be a primary selector of which customers receive a call, and this may drive neglect of other customers or higher-value activities. For example, most order holds may occur with smaller customers who collectively account for 15% of the receivables asset, diverting time from the customers who account for 85% of asset.

Another key determinant of the efficacy of the credit hold function is to monitor the volume of bad debt write-offs over several years. If the volume is unacceptably high, do not just automatically tighten the credit hold criteria for all customers and increase the workload. First determine how much of the bad debt loss would have been avoided with tighter credit hold criteria. In the example cited above, since Kmart was a major, national account, it is unlikely orders would have been held until late in the company's decline. Tighter credit hold criteria would only have generated more holds and manual releases, with no reduction in exposure.

Overall Risk Rating

Another control over the aggregate risk of the receivables asset is to compute an overall risk rating of the asset, based on the individual customer credit score or rating, and weighted by the percent of the total receivables controlled by each individual customer. This can be accomplished two ways:

1. By calculating a weighted credit score if you utilize credit scoring.
2. By calculating a weighted debt rating using the assigned debt ratings issued by commercial services such as Moody's, Standard & Poors, and so on. This approach is limited to customers who have publicly traded debt rated by agencies.

Metrics

The metrics to monitor the performance of the credit control function should be simple and require only several hours per month to compile and publish. They should address:

- Throughput and timeliness
- Effectiveness
- Cost

Throughput and timeliness metrics should measure the volume of credit investigations (new customers and updates of existing ones) and credit holds. In addition, they should report:

- Percent of applications denied, credit limits changed, and orders released without customer contact. This provides insight into the quality and benefit of these functions.

- Backlog (total and age of unprocessed items).

Note the metrics for credit holds can be compiled periodically for two-week periods to enable insight into the process. They do not have to be tracked continuously.

If the credit function has a commitment (or service-level agreement) to process credit applications for new customers within a specified time frame, that performance should also be measured and reported, simply as the percent of applications that were processed within the prescribed time period.

Effectiveness can be measured by the level of bad debt write-offs (actual charge-offs, not additions to the bad debt reserve) as a percent of revenue compared to the prior three years. Ensure the write-offs include only true bad debt and not concessions or credits and adjustments for disputes, billing errors, shipping problems, and so on. Another metric is the aggregate credit score of the receivables portfolio as measure of aggregate risk. A third metric could be the amount of revenue and its profitability sold to the lowest-rated segment of customers. This reveals the level of profitable sales made to high-risk customers and is an indicator of credit's responsibility to promote sales.

Cost can be measured by compiling the total cost of the function (the cost of purchased services and supplies, travel, etc., as well as personnel costs) and reporting it as a percent of revenue. World-class performance is for the credit and collection function combined to be 1/10 to 2/10 of 1 percent of revenue. The cost should also be reported compared to the budget for the current year.

Credit Insurance

Credit insurance insures against bad debt loss and can be a useful tool in controlling bad debt risk. It can limit exposure, but it has a cost. Credit insurance is offered by a number of firms and is available for both domestic and foreign customers. The coverage can be tailored to a company's individual needs. The typical offering has these features:

- Coverage applies only to customers approved by the insurer.
- Deductibles apply both on a per-occurrence and aggregate basis.
- A coinsurance provision applies.
- Premiums are based on the risk level of the portfolio and the strength of your internal credit controls as assessed by the insurer.
- Insurers want to insure the entire portfolio subject to their exclusions. They discourage covering only your high-risk customers, usually through high premiums, deductibles, and coinsurance.

While credit insurance can be very comforting, the cost/benefit trade-off must be closely evaluated. The evaluation can be completed in three steps:

1. Secure quotes from three providers, including an identification of which of your customers would be ineligible for coverage. Calculate the percentage of revenue sold to the ineligible customers.
2. Perform a modeling exercise in which you take the last three years of write-offs and compute how much these write-offs would have been reduced by the proposed credit insurance, net of deductibles, coinsurance, and premiums.
3. Forecast revenue and bad debt loss for the upcoming year. Calculate the reduction in bad debt loss covered by the insurance versus the total cost of the insurance. Include an estimate of bad debt loss for "ineligible" customers, that is, customers not covered by credit insurance. This loss rate should be higher than the historical aggregate rate as the ineligibles are the highest-risk customers.

This analysis will reveal if the total cost of the insurance is higher or lower than the historical/forecast bad debt loss covered by the insurance.

Export and Foreign Customers

In many respects, credit control over sales to offshore customers employs the same fundamentals discussed earlier in this chapter. Selling to large, financially strong customers in the European Union, Japan, and other countries can be conducted on open credit terms with little risk. Payment terms may be somewhat different to allow for transport of goods overseas or other local conditions. Remittances are usually made through wire transfers or other electronic means.

However, selling to smaller, less-well-capitalized firms or to firms of any size in developing countries entails a higher risk of loss. The risk may be slightly or much higher. The risk emanates from several factors:

- Lack of reliable financial and credit data on a customer.
- Foreign exchange risk. If you are to be paid in foreign currency, its value may decrease substantially from foreign exchange rate changes. Even if you are paid in U.S. dollars, an exchange rate change may make it expensive or difficult for a customer to obtain dollars and pay you.
- Political risk. Changes in local government may hurt the local economy or place restrictions on payment of U.S. dollars out of the country.
- Difficulty in enforcing your claims in the local legal system.

Many credit information services provide credit reporting and country risk information to enable credit decisions. The quality and reliability vary, and do not eliminate risk. The best credit information you can get is with an existing customer, for whom you have payment experience, and may be able to obtain audited financial statements. For new customers, the quality of the information is generally not what is desired, and the risk is elevated.

Mitigating credit risk on sales to offshore customers is a science in and of itself. There are numerous techniques and banking instruments to secure your claim and ensure payment. Several financing sources and government insurance programs are designed to promote exports (e.g., the Export Import Bank). Commercial credit insurance discussed above can be utilized. We will not attempt to cover them all. The best way to approach risk mitigation is to work with a bank or customs broker/exporter well versed in export payment instruments.

However, the simplest, most secure way to manage risk on export sales is to employ one or all of these techniques:

- Require full or partial payment in advance via a secure payment method, such as wire transfer of funds to your bank account.

- Require the customer to place a deposit with you to cover the exposure.

- Secure an irrevocable standby letter of credit, confirmed by a U.S. bank, for the anticipated exposure.

- Secure an irrevocable letter of credit, confirmed by a U.S. bank, for the amount of each order.

None of these methods will be popular with your customers. They will prefer open account terms. However, if there is a lack of reliable information to prove a low risk, this is the safest way to proceed. All other instruments for payment are less secure than the ones listed above. Over time, with experience with a customer, you may wish to sell smaller amounts on open credit to see if the customer pays on time. The open credit can be expanded with good payment history and access to company financial information.

Key Points

The four key points to remember about credit controls are:

1. Strong credit controls can make managing receivables much easier and less costly.

2. Credit decisions must be made quickly to avoid impeding customer response and to be cost effective.

3. Overly conservative credit policy and practice will constrain profitable sales.

4. The right credit controls must be customized to an individual company, its strategy, profitability, tolerance for risk, the nature of its customer base, and its products or services.

ORDER PROCESSING

Overview

Order processing is all about fulfilling a customer order properly, quickly, and invoicing it accurately. This creates a happy customer, and sets the stage for a prompt, full payment. Failure to fulfill and bill an order accurately guarantees a delayed and/or short payment, a dissatisfied customer, and the extra cost of reworking the order, processing a return, issuing a credit, reinvoicing, and so on. In other words, a mini-business disaster. The longer-term effect is to drive customers to the competition, which will fulfill and bill their order properly.

Order processing refers to the function of receiving a customer order, ensuring it meets the conditions of an acceptable order, and routing it within the company to be fulfilled. Speed is important, but filling the order to meet customer expectations is the primary mission and a determinant of the success or failure of a business.

Best Practice

Best Practice in order processing is to receive customer orders electronically (via Electronic Data Interchange [EDI] or other electronic means) and to route them electronically to the department within the company that will fulfill it. For a manufacturer or distributor of a tangible product, the order processing would automatically check inventory records for availability and print a pick list, packing slip, bill of lading, and so on, to enable the order to be prepared and shipped. For a services firm, it would involve assigning the order to a staff member to schedule to provide the service. Automatic routing eliminates the possibility of human error in transcription of the order for routing to fulfillment.

Before an order can be routed to fulfillment, it must be reviewed to ensure it meets the conditions of an acceptable order. Such conditions are elements such as:

- Price
- Freight terms (which party pays freight)
- Payment terms
- Delivery or completion date

If the order does not meet the acceptable options for these elements, an exception must be approved, or the customer must be notified of the unacceptable element of the order. Here again, Best Practice prescribes automatic reviews of orders and automatic routing of unacceptable ones to the proper approval authority.

Once the elements of the order are approved, the credit status of the customer must be checked before the order is released for fulfillment. If the customer's credit status is unacceptable, the order is placed on "credit hold," Best Practices for which were discussed in greater detail in the "Credit Controls" section.

Another condition of fulfilling an order is the validity of the order. In theory, it must be a bona fide order from an individual at the customer authorized to place orders. The customer often accomplishes this by placing a purchase order, which is a legal commitment to accept and pay for the order if it is satisfactorily fulfilled. Best Practice prescribes electronic placing of orders or releases of shipments against bulk or blanket purchase orders (usually through EDI). In the fast pace of commerce, many orders are placed via phone or e-mail, and only experience with each customer will determine if those orders are valid. Whatever form the order takes, it must have this information to be a valid order and to be fulfilled properly:

- A purchase order number. Most companies will not pay an invoice unless it references a valid purchase order.

- A clear description of the product or service ordered.
- Payment terms.
- Freight terms.
- Delivery date.
- Price.
- Quantity of product or service ordered.

The advantage of blanket purchase orders is that all of these elements are specified, and only the release quantity needs to be specified each time.

Once an order is deemed acceptable, it is routed to the appropriate fulfillment department within the company, where it is fulfilled, then invoiced. It is critically important that all the specifications of the order are received accurately and routed accurately, so the customer will be billed accurately. Best Practice prescribes electronic communication of this information to minimize transcription errors.

Key Points

The two important points to remember about order processing are to:

1. Fill the order correctly and promptly.
2. Bill it accurately.

When both these steps are consistently achieved, delinquent receivables are minimized, and the cost of managing the asset is reduced.

INVOICING

Overview

The purpose of presenting an invoice (also called billing) to a customer is to secure payment for having provided a product or service (or as a deposit on the future provision of a product or service). The invoicing function in many companies is highly automated, requires little manual intervention, and is often overlooked. However, *invoicing accuracy is the single most important determinant of effective and efficient receivables management.*

Accurate invoicing has been the central theme in our discussions of the quotation, contract administration, pricing, and order processing functions. Accuracy in billing cannot be achieved unless the aforementioned functions are performed properly.

Accurate invoicing directly drives:

- Lower receivables delinquency and increased cash flow
- Reduced exposure to bad debt loss
- Lower cost of administering the entire revenue cycle
- Fewer concessions of disputed items
- Enhanced customer service and satisfaction

In fact, many customers, in rating their vendors, measure invoice accuracy. The reason is that inaccurate invoices raise their internal cost of paying bills and, therefore, are part of the total cost of buying from a vendor.

The two key objectives of invoicing are *accuracy* and *speed*. Accuracy is defined as meeting the customer's requirements for timely payment of an invoice. Companies often complain how difficult it is to conduct business with government agencies or with large, bureaucratic companies,

▶ **CASE HISTORY** ◀

Inaccurate Billing Loses the Bid

A New England distributor was bidding on an annual supply contract with a major customer. After devoting an enormous amount of time and expense in preparing the bid and cutting prices, it was disappointed to learn that the contract was awarded to a competitor. The reason given was that even though this distributor had the lowest quoted price, its billing inaccuracy hurt its vendor rating and raised the customer's total cost of buying the company's products.

citing slow payments. While it is true that accurate invoices are sometimes lost or paid slowly, the predominant cause of delinquent receivables from this type of customer is *failing to meet their invoicing requirements*. Often a government agency or large customer's invoicing requirements may be different from the majority of customers. You may feel that the requirements are outdated, unnecessary, or arcane, but in order to receive timely payment, *they must be met*. Even if customized processing is required to generate an invoice that meets requirements, it is usually worth the extra expense, especially since you will end up producing a "customized" invoice in the resolution of a dispute.

Speed is defined as presenting an invoice to the customer as soon as permissible under the terms of the business agreement (usually after shipping a product, rendering a service, or achieving a milestone). Invoice presentation can be accelerated by electronic presentation. Many companies begin the countdown to the due date on receipt of the vendor invoice, so speed of invoicing is critical to maximize receivables asset turnover. Speed, however, is less important than accuracy, as an inaccurate invoice will typically delay payment by several weeks. A

▶ CASE HISTORY ◀

Accuracy over Speed

A supplier of medical devices usually delivered its product directly to the operating room within a hospital. The hospital's preferred practice was to generate the purchase order after delivery so the exact quantity and type of product used would be known. Although the supplier was able to generate an invoice one day after delivery, it delayed invoicing until it received the purchase order (PO) number from the hospital. Often the purchase order number was secured 10 days beyond product delivery. In this case, however, delayed billing was the proper choice, because an invoice without a PO number would be rejected by the hospital's payables group. The rejection would not be discovered until at least 35 days beyond invoice date, and correction of the problem could take another 10 to 15 days.

As this example illustrates, accuracy in invoicing is more important than speed.

delay of a few days to ensure accuracy is worth the avoidance of weeks of delay caused by a disputed invoice.

A useful way to measure invoicing accuracy is with the Billing Quality Index (BQI). The BQI is calculated by dividing the non–error-based credit memos or adjustments processed during a period of time by the number of invoices issued in that same time period. For example, if a company issued 10,000 invoices and 700 non–error-based credit memos during the second quarter of 2004, its BQI would be 7%. Viewed another way, a 7% BQI means that 7%, or 1 of approximately every 14 invoices, is later corrected with a credit memo. Let us examine the implications of this 7% BQI.

An accurate invoice will usually be paid by the customer around the due date with no further effort or perhaps one collection follow-up reminder. An inaccurate invoice will generate at least one collection follow-up, then an investigation into the dispute, resolution, and correction via issuing a credit memo. Resolution of an inaccurate invoice will require much more time and can impact several individuals. The cost of issuing a credit memo is estimated at $100 to $200; the cost of an invoice is only several dollars. In addition, there is the interest cost of receivables delinquency of the inaccurate invoice.

So if 1 of every 14 invoices requires the extra cost and effort just mentioned, in a high-invoice-volume environment, this will be a serious cost and delinquency problem.

A BQI under 3% is acceptable performance. Years ago, when Xerox Corporation won the Malcolm Baldrige Award for quality, it cited a 2% BQI, with intentions of achieving 1%. A 2% BQI means 1 of every 50 invoices requires correction. That is a much lower cost profile than the 1-of-14 invoice scenario discussed above.

Exhibit 2.1 illustrates the calculation and graphical presentation of the BQI.

Best Practice

There are five Best Practices for order processing.

1. The compilation of the correct information to trigger and populate an invoice is specific to the system application used for

Exhibit 2.1   Billing Quality Index

	Number	Percent to Invoice	Value $(000)	Percent to Invoice
Credit Memos	13,488	7.55	2,230	6.77
Invoices	178,716		32,940	

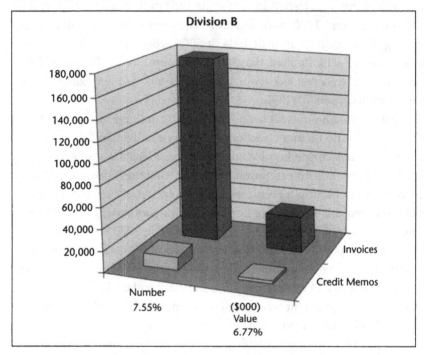

order processing and billing. For our purposes, it is sufficient to note that the system gathers information from the contract, pricing, customer master, shipping, time/service expense, and other files to generate an invoice. Best Practice is for the invoice to clearly display this information:

- Bill-to address: customer company name, address.
- Bill-to approval authority (where applicable) or department (accounts payable) at the customer to whom the invoice must go.
- Ship-to address.

- Invoice number and date.
- Customer account number.
- Vendor federal tax identification number.
- Customer purchase order number.
- Date product shipped or service delivered.
- Vendor internal sales order number.
- Quantity and description of product or service delivered. (This must appear in layman's terms and not be engineering jargon or abbreviations. Remember, an accounts payable clerk is going to determine if the invoice is for the product/service ordered on the PO.)
- Unit price(s).
- Extended amount(s) due (quantity × unit price).
- Discounts (price only, not prompt payment discounts).
- Freight and sales tax if applicable.
- Total amount due.
- Payment terms.
- Due date.
- Remittance address (post office box or lockbox for regular mail, street address of lockbox for courier deliveries, and bank information for wire transfers and other electronic payments).
- Phone number (and/or name) of person to call if the customer has a question about the invoice, with phrase "Questions about this invoice should be directed to. ..."
- Tear-off remittance portion, with instructions to include invoice number, amount paid for each invoice, customer account number, how to pay with a credit or procurement card, a change of address section, and any Optical Character Readable (OCR) number or bar code for scanning. Also include a request to return the remittance portion or list the information on the check or electronic payment.

- Boldface message in large font, stating "Please pay $xxxx.yy" by month, day, year."

- Offer of prompt payment discount (if any), phrased: "Save $xx.yy if payment received by discount month, day, year."

- Late payment fee/finance charge statement.

- Attachments as required by customer.

- Invoice should have a header similar to vendor company letterhead, showing name, address, logo.

- The phrase "Original Invoice" should appear on the invoice.

  To ensure your invoice is easy to handle, put yourself in the shoes of the accounts payable clerk who has to review the invoice and match it to a PO and receiving document. The invoice should be clear, easy to read, highlight the most important information, and convey a message of what action you want (i.e., pay in full by specified date to lockbox).

2. Best Practice is to present invoices electronically (Electronic Data Interchange [EDI], Electronic Invoice Presentation and Payment [EIPP], or other electronic means), to bill as quickly as possible, and to ensure it is accepted by the customer. If a customer claims not to have received invoices, it is prudent to check the electronic confirmation of receipt with a phone call to the customer to ensure the invoices were routed to the proper department within the customer.

3. Unbilled receivables are receivables where the service or product has been delivered, the revenue has been recognized, but the invoice has not been generated. Best Practice is to minimize unbilled receivables. Receivables management is rife with uncertainty. When an invoice is delivered to a customer, it is not completely certain if it will ever be paid, and it is very uncertain when it will be paid. However, there is no uncertainty with unbilled receivables. *They will never be paid.*

   Earlier we stated that accuracy is more important than speed in invoicing. Having said that, the level of unbilled receivables must be constantly monitored and managed so it can be mini-

▶ **CASE HISTORY** ◀

Information Technology Bug Stops Payments

A large manufacturer of food products conducted most of its business with the large supermarket chains via EDI, receiving purchase orders and presenting invoices electronically. One supermarket chain that usually paid its invoices on time started to fall behind and grew a significant past due balance. When contacted, the customer's payables department stated that the invoices had not been received. After research by the customer's information technology (IT) department, it was discovered that although a confirmation of receipt was received from the customer when the invoices were transmitted, internal IT problems prevented the invoices from being routed to accounts payable.

mized. Unbilled receivables occur most frequently in service industries, where service is rendered, but invoices are generated weekly or, in extreme cases, monthly. Accelerating accurate billing will increase cash flow.

4. Correcting inaccurate invoices is usually accomplished four ways:

a. Issuing a credit memo for the incorrect amount

b. Instructing the customer to short pay the invoice, then processing an adjustment for the difference

c. Issuing a corrected "original" invoice, that is, an invoice with the same invoice number as the original, incorrect one

d. Issuing a credit memo for the entire amount of the inaccurate invoice, and rebilling the correct amount under a new invoice number

Best Practice is ultimately to correct an invoice in a manner acceptable to the customer that will result in the correct amount being paid as early as possible. Best Practice is also to try to influence the customer to correct the inaccurate invoice in the manner that is the least work for you. This can be accomplished by offering your preferred resolution to the customer. Option b above is the simplest way to correct an inaccurate invoice, although there are audit trail risks, and the adjustment may not be recorded accurately in the accounting records. Option a is the cleanest from an accounting and control perspective, but involves creation of a credit memo. Options c and d can involve confusion over invoice numbers and original invoice dates.

5. Best Practice also includes improving invoicing accuracy on a continuous basis. As stated earlier, the rewards of accurate invoicing are enormous, and as business changes, new sources of error will continually arise. A formal program of improving billing quality using Six Sigma, Total Quality Management, or other methodology is an integral part of Best Practice in receivables management. Utilization of dispute and/or credit memo causality data is essential to direct the continuous improvement efforts, and to measure the progress.

Customer Satisfaction Assurance

It is often beneficial to use special handling for very large value invoices to ensure their accuracy, delivery, receipt, and agreement by the customer. This helps to ensure prompt payment of large invoices, and it also enhances customer service. The definition of a "large" invoice will vary by company. The customer satisfaction assurance process couches the collection objective within a customer service approach.

The objectives of the customer satisfaction assurance process are to:

- Ensure customer satisfaction with the large purchase
- Promptly identify and quickly resolve disputes
- Ensure timely payment of the large invoice

The customer satisfaction assurance process must be tailored to an individual business. The next example illustrates how the process works for a capital equipment manufacturer. For simplicity, we will exclude any down payment or deposits, which are common to these

► CASE HISTORY ◄

Special Handling Required

A publisher of legal reference books typically sold one set of reference materials at a time to its hundreds of thousands of customers. Individual order sizes were approximately $1,200. However, a few large county court systems would purchase in bulk and distribute the materials themselves. Invoices to these customers totaled over $100,000. Clearly, these invoices merited special handling and attention as their payment was equal to that from 80 to 100 average invoices. The customer satisfaction assurance process is perfect for these county court system customers.

Note: The county court customers required consolidated invoices. Although this required the vendor to manually prepare (i.e., type) the consolidated invoices, it enabled the invoices to be paid on time, which brought a huge cash flow benefit to the vendor. Customized processing is often warranted for large customers.

transactions. The focus is on the large, final invoice. The two basic steps would be:

1. After receipt of the order and several weeks prior to shipment and presentation of the original invoice:

    a. Make proactive and repeated confirmation with the customer of the order specifications, equipment configuration, delivery date, price, and payment terms. This communication should be presented to the customer as proactive customer service to ensure that the order is filled exactly to requirements. Any discrepancies between the customer's purchase order and the quotation should also be resolved during this time period before shipment. In addition to providing excellent service to customers who order big-ticket items, this step identifies any discrepancies and communicates your expectation of the settlement of the transaction. The customer is informed that you are expecting the full amount of the invoice to be paid on a specified due date. In some cases, this can uncover a customer's intention to lease the equipment rather than pay in full. Since arranging a lease requires weeks, the earlier this financing intention is discovered, the sooner you will get paid by the lessor.

b. Issue a pro forma invoice that clearly states the amount and due date of the payment. It should also include all the other informational contents of a good invoice as listed above. The pro forma invoice should be reviewed with the customer to ensure their understanding and to secure a commitment to pay the full amount on the due date.

2. Postshipment and generation of the original invoice

a. Deliver the invoice electronically or via overnight courier.

b. Confirm receipt of the invoice and the customer's agreement with it a few days after it is delivered. This will identify any disputes early, so resolution can begin. Again, this should be couched in terms of a customer service call. Inquire about the status of the installation of the equipment and if there are any issues, but work toward the invoice and payment subject. All issues identified should be routed to service or sales for remediation.

c. A few days before the invoice due date, confirm that payment has been made or scheduled.

d. Follow-up in short intervals until the invoice has been paid.

Key Points

There are five key points regarding invoicing:

1. Accuracy is the Holy Grail of invoicing. It drives efficiency and effectiveness in the entire revenue cycle.

2. The content and format of the invoice is important:
    *   Make it easy to process.
    *   Make it clear what you expect (i.e., *full payment by due date*).

> ▶ **CASE HISTORY** ◀

Customer Satisfaction Assurance Gets Results

A multibillion-dollar (sales) computer manufacturer derived a substantial portion of its revenue from sales of large, integrated computer hardware systems. It would not invoice until the equipment was delivered and installed, but when the invoice was issued, its payment terms were "due upon receipt." In the past, the company's practice was to treat "due upon receipt" terms as net 30 day terms. Collection follow-up would commence on these large invoices 35 days from invoice date. If a dispute was raised, or if the invoice was not received, resolution of the issue would not begin until 35 days beyond invoice date. This resulted in payments being received in 35 days for a sale with no issues to hundreds of days for sales with multiple issues. After implementing the customer satisfaction assurance process for all orders over $200,000, the company realized the following results:

- Forty percent of the sales of large systems were paid within 20 days of invoice date, versus only 12% previously.
- The average payment period for all large system invoices was cut in half within six months.

This result demonstrates the effectiveness of the customer satisfaction assurance process. It also demonstrates that "due upon receipt" terms are not equivalent to net 30 day terms. You can get a significant number of customers to pay earlier than 30 days if you actively pursue payment prior to 30 days from invoice date.

3. Deliver invoices electronically.

4. Minimize unbilled revenue, but do not sacrifice accuracy (see Holy Grail).

5. Utilize the customer satisfaction assurance process for the big-ticket billings.

Note

1. Bankruptcy Data.com, New Generation Research, Inc.

CHAPTER 3

Receivables Asset Management

INTRODUCTION

Management of the receivables asset begins when all of the antecedent functions are completed and a receivable is posted to the detailed accounts receivable ledger (a comprehensive list of all amounts owed the company). The receivables begin aging immediately, increasing the cost of financing them and increasing the risk of nonpayment. Now what?

Management of this asset (which is one of the largest assets of the company) involves safeguarding the asset and accelerating cash inflow (increasing asset turnover). If you view this asset as a vault of cash, think of the precautions a bank takes to protect its cash reserves. However, receivables are much more fluid and an integral part of doing business, so the safeguarding and acceleration of turnover must be accomplished:

- At low cost
- Without strangling sales volume
- Without alienating customers and colleagues.

This chapter presents Best Practices for achieving this difficult task.

PORTFOLIO STRATEGY

Overview

An old joke provides insight into how to manage a receivables asset. The joke starts with the question, "How do you eat an elephant?" The answer: "One bite at a time."

A receivables portfolio strategy defines the approach to managing the receivables. It answers the question, "How am I going to manage this asset?" It starts with breaking the entire asset into "bite-size" pieces. It is absolutely essential to know the size and makeup of a receivables asset (or portfolio) before you can design a strategy and marshal the required resources to manage it.

Best Practices

Developing a portfolio strategy is a step-by-step process.

STEP ONE—Analyze the Size, Composition, and Complexity of the Receivables Portfolio.

To illustrate, consider two different receivables portfolios, each with a value of $1 billion. An aircraft manufacturer like Boeing could have 5 customers and 8 to 10 open invoices for aircraft (excluding spare parts and service revenue invoices for simplicity's sake). A food distributor such as Sysco could have over a million customers and tens of millions of open invoices. A vastly different portfolio strategy is required for each of these two portfolios. Begin the analysis by examining:

- The number of customer accounts.

- The number and value of open line items inclusive of invoices, credit memos, unapplied payments, and other debits and credits.

- The concentration of receivables. Is a large portion of the value of the portfolio controlled by a relatively few accounts? Often you will find that the Pareto principle (the 80/20 rule) applies; that is, 80% of the receivables are controlled by 20% of the customers. The degree of concentration has critically important implications for how the asset is best managed.

Exhibits 3.1 and 3.2 illustrate the concentration analysis.

The complexity of the receivables portfolio is a function of two major factors:

1. The complexity of the business and the vulnerability of its invoices to dispute by customers. An illustration of this concept is to contrast an invoice for a shipment of copier paper to an invoice for the completion of a consulting project milestone. The copier paper invoice is subject to dispute for quantity, price, or damage/quality. The consulting invoice is vulnerable to a very subjective interpretation of whether the milestone was achieved, and the time, consultant and customer work hours required, overall satisfaction with the engagement, level of travel expense, and so on. The consulting business has a much higher complexity, and therefore it is more difficult to manage the receivables asset.

2. The level of "clutter" in the portfolio. Clutter is defined as all types of open transactions except whole open invoices. Clutter transactions include:

    - Short-paid invoices (deductions)
    - Credit memos
    - Unapplied payments
    - Unearned discount chargebacks
    - Late payment fees (finance or service charges)
    - Other chargebacks, billbacks, or debit memos
    - Other adjustments or credits

The reason clutter increases complexity is that it obscures the true amount owed by the customer, can confuse the customer, and/or precipitates dispute over the amount owed. In contrast, the collection of a whole, open invoice begins as a simple collection contact. An un-

Exhibit 3.1 Receivables Portfolio Concentration

This portfolio is very concentrated. Instead of the rule of thumb of 20% of customers controlling 80% of receivables value, just 10% of customers control 82% of the value. To manage this asset, you really need to focus only on the top 169 to 306 accounts, not all 1,628 customers. Such concentration cuts the size of the task significantly.

Total Account Balance	Per Stratum				Cumulative			
	# of Accounts	% of Total	A/R ($000)	% of Total	# of Accounts	% of Total	A/R ($000)	% of Total
>$1,000,000	49	3.0	133,962	56.8	49	3.0	133,692	56.8
$500,000–$999,999	49	3.0	34,086	14.4	98	6.0	168,048	71.2
$250,000–$499,999	71	4.4	24,882	10.5	169	10.4	192,930	81.8
$100,000–$249,999	137	4.4	22,095	9.4	306	18.8	215,025	91.1
$50,000–$99,999	143	8.8	9,925	4.2	449	27.6	224,950	95.3
$25,000–$49,999	210	12.0	7,280	3.1	659	40.5	232,229	98.4
$10,000–$24,999	278	17.1	4,542	1.9	937	57.6	236,772	100.4
$5,000–$9,999	199	12.2	1,460	0.6	1136	69.8	238,231	101.0
$1,000–$4,999	261	16.0	711	0.3	1397	85.8	238,942	101.3
$500–$999	82	5.0	62	0.0	1479	90.8	239,004	101.3
< $500	102	6.3	25	0.0	1581	97.1	239,029	101.3
Credit Balance	47	2.9	(3,104)	–1.3	1628	100.0	235,926	100.0
Total	1628	100.0	235,926	100.0				

56

Exhibit 3.2 Receivables Portfolio Concentration

This division of a company had a fairly typical concentration: 22% of customers controlled 83% of receivables. That is very close to the 80/20 rule of thumb.

Total Account Balance	Per Stratum				Cumulative			
	# of Accounts	% of Total	A/R ($000)	% of Total	# of Accounts	% of Total	A/R ($000)	% of Total
> $100,000	1	0.1	270	6.7	1	0.1	270	6.7
$50,000–99,999.99	3	0.2	184	4.6	4	0.2	454	11.3
$25,000–49,999.99	18	1.1	614	15.2	22	1.3	1,068	26.5
$10,000–$24,999.00	63	3.7	892	22.1	85	5.0	1,960	48.7
$5,000–$9,999.99	106	6.3	741	18.4	191	11.3	2,701	67.0
$2,500–$4,999.99	180	10.7	621	15.4	371	22.0	3,322	82.5
$1,000–$2,499.99	312	18.5	515	12.8	683	40.5	3,838	95.3
$500–$999.99	241	14.3	174	4.3	924	54.7	4,011	99.6
$250–$499.99	207	12.3	75	1.9	1131	67.0	4,086	101.4
$100–$249.99	219	13.0	37	0.9	1350	80.0	4,124	102.4
$50–$99.99	86	5.1	6	0.2	1436	85.1	4,130	102.5
$1–$24.99	6	0.4	0	0.0	1509	89.4	4,133	102.6
0	10	0.6	0	0.0	1519	90.0	4,133	102.6
< 0 (credit balance)	169	10.0	(104)	–2.6	1688	100.0	4,029	100.0
Total	1688	100.0	4,029	100.0				

57

derlying dispute may be identified, but often the contact revolves around when the invoice will be paid, not if and how much. However, dealing with clutter requires significant time and discussion trying to establish the amount owed, not when it will be paid. Often it triggers additional research and provision of documentation before the topic of when payment will be made is even broached. Clutter increases the difficulty of collection.

Exhibits 3.3 and 3.4 illustrate the clutter concept. Note the number of clutter transactions in these two portfolios. Every one of them will have to be cleared from the ledger at some point. How much time and effort will be required? Inevitably, it will be a lot more than the time and effort required to clear the whole open invoices.

The portfolio in Exhibit 3.3 is relatively simple to manage. Most of the open transactions are large, whole open invoices, with modest amounts of clutter. Matching and clearing of the unapplied cash would clear many open invoices and make the task of managing the portfolio easier.

STEP TWO—Segment the Portfolio.

The portfolio can be segmented according to a variety of attributes:

- Size of customer determined by sales volume or open receivables

Exhibit 3.3   Receivables Portfolio Components

This portfolio is relatively simple to manage. Most of the open transactions are large, whole open invoices, with modest amounts of clutter. Matching and clearing of the unapplied cash would clear many open invoices and make the task of managing the portfolio easier.

Transactions	Number Open	Value Open ($000)	Average Value ($)
Whole open invoices	6,459	213,362	33,033
Short-paid invoices	446	7,241	16,235
Unapplied cash	539	(18,667)	(34,633)
Miscellaneous credits	49	(394)	(8,041)
Total	7,493	201,542	N.A.

Exhibit 3.4   Receivables Portfolio Components

This service company had over 16,000 clutter transactions. If it takes five minutes of work to clear one clutter transaction, it would require eight to nine months for one person to clear this clutter.

Transaction	Number	Total ($)	Average ($)
Whole invoices	40,339	9,075,113	225
Deductions	14,147	1,016,609	72
Whole credit memos	671	(270,067)	(402)
Partial credit memos	91	(38,027)	(418)
Whole debit memos	207	30,225	146
Partial debit memos	32	1,258	39
Whole unapplied payments	493	(473,618)	(961)
Partial unapplied payments	734	(225,558)	(307)
Total	56,714	9,115,934	161

- Private versus public sector
- Domestic versus foreign based
- Line of business or division
- Open account versus cash on delivery or letter of credit
- Risk rating or payment history
- Type of customer: distributor/dealer versus end user.
- Alignment with sales force
- Geography or time zone
- Profitability

The key criterion to determine how to define a segment is to answer the question: Does the segment as defined merit a tailored approach to managing its receivables? If the answer is yes, then a segment should be defined.

What do we mean by a "tailored approach to managing the receivables"? It is unwise to treat all customers the same. Customers vary in importance to your company, in how they operate, and their relative risk vs. profitability. Here are some examples:

- You would not treat Procter & Gamble (P&G) the same way you would treat a small, start-up organic soap manufacturer. You would make more frequent collection calls with the start-up and withhold shipments as needed. The approach with P&G would be to work with it to maintain the account, communicate mostly by e-mail, and rarely, if ever, even consider holding shipments.

- You would be more willing to bear risk with a highly profitable customer than with a marginally profitable customer.

- The approach to a large retailer would be focused more on processing deductions than pursuing past due open invoices.

- The communication path for a customer where invoices require a signature approval in lieu of a receiving document (for a service) would be different from a customer who matches the invoice with a receiving document (for a tangible product).

- The approach to a government customer would be different from a private sector customer.

STEP THREE—*Formulate an Approach for Specific Segments.*

Once the segments are defined, then formulate an approach or strategy for effectively and efficiently managing the receivables owed by that segment. The approach will define the amount of effort, resource, and tools required and the required skill sets of the staff. For example, if Segment 1 is thousands of small, thinly capitalized but moderately profitable customers, the strategy may entail:

- High volume of automated, progressively more stern collection letters

- High volume of collection calls firmly stressing the need to pay quickly to avoid service interruption

- Automated order and shipment hold when credit limit or delinquency thresholds are violated

- Low-resource, low-cost receivables management

This segment should be managed to minimize bad debt loss. The collector skills required to manage this segment are the ability to make a very high volume of effective collection calls each day. The ability to reconcile customer accounts and handle disputes is much less important.

For another example, Segment 2 consists of a few very large, very creditworthy customers who account for a substantial portion of total revenue and profit. Here the strategy might entail:

- An account maintenance approach to collection, providing supporting documentation (invoice copy, proof of delivery) for skipped invoices

- Friendly reminders on past due invoices

- Prompt, high-volume deduction processing

- Frequent account reconciliation and cleanup efforts

- Periodic face-to-face meetings with purchasing and accounts payable

- Higher levels of customer service, and a higher cost to service and maintain the account and the relationship

- Order holds only by exception in extreme circumstances

This segment should be managed to generate maximum cash flow while controlling deduction and concession losses. A significant slowdown of payments from this customer segment will have a major impact on the firm's cash flow. The collector skills required to manage this segment are a thorough understanding of customer accounting, account reconciliation and maintenance, deduction and adjustment processing, document retrieval, and the ability to establish a good working rapport with customer payables staff and with internal sales staff.

Formulation of a strategy involves deciding:

- The primary objective for managing the segment (i.e., cash flow or bad debt minimization or combination of the two)

- The type and frequency of customer contact (calls, collection letters, statements, face to face meetings, reconciliation packs)

- The amount of and type of resource to manage the segment (collectors, sales or customer service staff, third-party collection agencies, etc.) and the skill sets required

- The appropriate use of credit hold and other security devices (guarantees, letters of credit, liens, etc).

An excellent tool for formulating a collection strategy for each portfolio segment is the collection intensity matrix. It enables you to display the portfolio segments and cryptically describe the approach to each segment. Exhibit 3.5 illustrates a collection intensity matrix.

In total, the portfolio in Exhibit 3.5 has 1,688 customer accounts. One option would be to plan how to manage 1,688 accounts with the same approach. This option would require two or three collectors. The segmentation shown in the exhibit, based only on the size of the receivables balance, provides insight into an alternative strategy. Note that accounts with balances over $5,000 control 67% of the portfolio value. Another option (or strategy) would be to have one collector manage it in this way:

- Devote at least half of his or her time to the A accounts. The A segment is managed to maximize cash flow. Remember, a portion of the 191 A accounts will pay their invoices on time, so it will not be necessary to call all 191.

- Devote at least one quarter of his or her time to the B accounts, which control 28% of the receivables value. This portfolio is less concentrated than others, so the B segment requires significant attention.

- For the C segment, monitor the timely issuance of the collection letters (by mail or e-mail), respond to incoming calls elicited by

Exhibit 3.5 Collection Intensity Matrix

Level	Percent of A/R	Number of Accounts	Invoice Date	Due Date	Due Date +30	Due Date +60
A. Cash Flow	67% (>$5K)	191	⊢ Proactive Calls ⊣	Periodic Meetings	⊢ Frequent Calling ⊣ / Escalate →	
B. Combination	28% ($1–5K)	492	⊢ Proactive Calls on Large Inventories ⊣	⊢ Collection Calls ⊣	Escalate →	
C. Bad Debt Avoidance	5% (<$1K)	826		⊢ Collection Letters Series ⊣	⊢ Collection Calls ⊣ / Escalate →	
D. Credit Balance		179				Credit Hold →

63

the letters, and perform collection calls only on accounts that are substantially past due (30 to 45 days). These calls should be of a more urgent nature than calls made to less past due accounts. Credit hold should be invoked without delay. This will enable the C segment to be managed to minimize bad debt loss on a very low-cost basis.

- Assign the 179 D accounts to administrative support to issue refunds or match to related accounts as appropriate, as time permits.

This sample portfolio strategy illustrates how to:

- Segment a portfolio
- Formulate a different approach for each segment
- Determine the resources required for each segment given the approach

Note the example assumes the existence of an automated collection letter capability and administrative support available to the collector. However, it also demonstrates how a seemingly large portfolio of 1,688 accounts requiring multiple collectors can be well managed with one collector and some administrative support.

The primary skill set required is effective collection calling. The caller must also be a well-organized, high-output worker.

The next case studies show how different companies used portfolio strategies, identified segments, and formulated approaches to them. Some of these examples may be applicable to your receivables asset or trigger thoughts on how to best segment and manage it.

▶ CASE HISTORY ◀

Super Customer Strategy

A Southwest service company had a single customer that controlled one-third of total receivables, generally paid promptly, and took a high volume of deductions (many of which were invalid). The port-

Case History *(continued)*

folio strategy for this company defined the super customer as a segment by itself. The objective was to minimize invalid deductions (a direct reduction of revenue) and to quickly secure payment on skipped invoices, which had a significant cash flow effect. The approach was to quickly follow up on skipped invoices, process deductions and promptly chargeback and collect the invalid ones, and conduct periodic account reconciliation meetings. Several staff members were devoted to this segment, and senior management's help was enlisted for the periodic meetings.

The remainder of the customers were segmented into public sector vs. private sector accounts. The public sector accounts were delegated to a collector with experience and knowledge in government payment processes. The private sector customers were managed with a high-volume calling at 30 days past due, supported by automated collection letters and automatic credit hold on orders at 45 days past due.

► **CASE HISTORY** ◄

Concentrated Portfolio Strategy

A West Coast manufacturer of medical devices had a very concentrated portfolio. Instead of the usual 80/20 distribution, this firm had a 76/6 distribution, meaning 76% of the receivables were controlled by only 6% of customers. The top 6% (which totaled 341 customers) were defined as a separate segment. The objective of the segment approach was to manage these customers for cash flow through high-intensity, short-interval collection contact where needed, periodic account reconciliation, and face-to-face meetings. The resources assigned were the company's best, senior collectors, supported by administrative staff. The remaining segments, which controlled 24% of the asset value, were comprised of over 5,000 customers. These were allocated to two segments: medium and small. Both segments were managed for bad debt avoidance, employing a high-contact volume approach, supported by credit hold at 60 days past due. The medium-size customers were given a higher priority.

▶ CASE HISTORY ◀

Cleaning Up Deductions

A manufacturer of consumer products that sold to major retail and supermarket chains had only 450 customers, with a typical 80/20 concentration. The majority of customers were well capitalized and paid invoices promptly. However, an analysis of the composition of the receivables portfolio revealed that 75% of the open transactions were deductions. The portfolio was segmented by geography to align collectors with the sales organization, which was also geographically deployed. The approach was to follow up on skipped invoices, process deductions, and reconcile/maintain the accounts to clear clutter. When face-to-face meetings were warranted, the collector and sales representative would team up. The staff members deployed to the accounts were skilled in deduction research/resolution and account reconciliation. Collection calling skills were secondary.

Key Points

The four key questions to answer when developing a portfolio strategy are:

1. What are the logical segments that require a different approach to be managed optimally?

2. What are the major components of the approach: which actions, timing, and so on?

3. What are the skill sets needed to implement the approach?

4. How many staff members and what tools and support are needed?

COLLECTION PROCESS

Overview

The collection process executes the portfolio strategy for each segment. To achieve best results, the collection process should vary by segment.

Examples of how the process can be varied were presented in the preceding section.

Best Practices

While elements of the collection process should be tailored to each portfolio segment, there are tools and techniques that are common to all or most segments.

Collection Timeline

The starting point for the collection process of each segment is the collection timeline, also known as an escalation protocol. The collection timeline defines which steps are taken at which points in time and by whom in both:

- The normal collection process
- The increasingly severe actions that will be taken with a customer who is seriously past due

It is important that this timeline is agreed to by all of senior management, so that when it is time to invoke its more severe remedies, sales, general management, and finance present a united front to the customer.

Exhibit 3.6 is an illustration of a collection timeline.

► CASE HISTORY ◄

Need to Prioritize Large Customers

A manufacturer of apparel sold to over 10,000 customers. The receivables portfolio was relatively concentrated, but contained thousands of small customers with receivable balances under $1,000. The collection staff did not differentiate between large and small customers, preferring to treat all customers the same. As a result, the collectors spent well over half their time on small balances, while large past due balances were not addressed. Cash flow, delinquency, and days sales outstanding (DSO) all suffered.

Exhibit 3.6   Collection Timeline

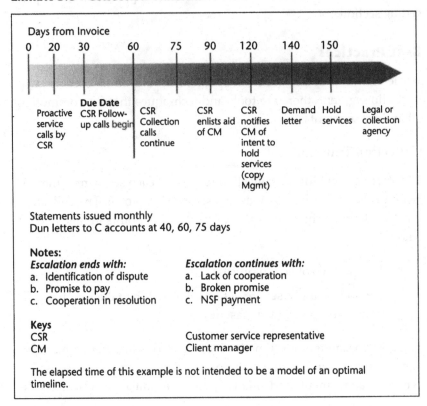

Statements issued monthly
Dun letters to C accounts at 40, 60, 75 days

Notes:

Escalation ends with:
a. Identification of dispute
b. Promise to pay
c. Cooperation in resolution

Escalation continues with:
a. Lack of cooperation
b. Broken promise
c. NSF payment

Keys
CSR   Customer service representative
CM   Client manager

The elapsed time of this example is not intended to be a model of an optimal timeline.

Customer Contact Timing

The timing of customer contact is an integral part of the collection process. The general rule of thumb for collection contact is: More (contact) is better than less, and earlier (contact) is better than later.

Prompt enforcement of payment terms is a Best Practice that improves results (cash flow, bad debt exposure, etc.) and educates customers of your expectations. A good basic posture is to expect every penny to be paid by the due date. In reality, that will not occur, but it is a good way to approach the management of the receivables asset. Prompt enforcement means calling on large accounts three to four days past the due date. Even terms of "due upon receipt" or "net 7 days" can be managed this way. Many collection departments concede 30 days on these payment terms. It is true that an increasing number of companies have set minimums of 30, 45, or 60 days for paying invoices. Securing exceptions for your firm is difficult and usually requires senior management involvement. However, for customers without ironclad rules, if "due upon receipt" and "net 7 day" terms are pursued with an expectation they will be paid in the next check run, 20 to 30% of these invoices can be paid in significantly less than 30 days. This can have a substantial impact on the overall receivables management results.

Another Best Practice for collection contact is proactive collection contact; that is, calling the customer prior to the due date. The major benefit of this approach is to identify problems with an invoice prior to the due date, in the hope they can be resolved quickly and payment received within terms. The classic example of this is the customer's accounts payable group not having the invoice. An invoice can be sent in a few minutes. Why wait for an invoice to be 5 to 10 days past due before finding out the customer does not have it? If this problem is identified and resolved 10 days prior to the due date, it is highly likely that the payment will be received within terms.

The basic principles of proactive collection contact are:

- It is customer service–oriented, to promptly identify and resolve any discrepancies with the order fulfillment or invoice. If no problems exist, inquire if the invoice is scheduled to be paid by the due date.
- It occurs prior to the due date, so resolution can be effected to ensure that payment can be received by the due date. It also educates the customer that you are serious about enforcing your payment terms.
- It is still a collection call. Ask for the payment on the due date.

Proactive contact should be focused on large balance accounts, as it is more time consuming than a "straight" collection call on past due invoices.

Some customers will balk at answering questions about invoices not yet past due. One way to overcome this objection is to point out the desire to service and maintain the customer's account and to help resolve any problem. Resolution starts with identification. Some will be strongly resentful and may have to be exempted from proactive contact.

A good way to start proactive contact is to call customers with some past due invoices. Inquire about the past due invoices first, then inquire about a few large individual invoices that will become due within 10 days. Over time, proactive contact can be expanded to the majority of the large accounts, addressing large invoices 10 to 15 days from the due date. Ultimately, the goal is to migrate to a total account management approach, reviewing past due and almost due invoices, as well as any "clutter" that needs to be cleared.

A suggested script for proactive collection contact is:

- Have you received the invoice?
- Is it in order?
- When is it scheduled for payment?
- If acceptable, confirm the commitment to pay on a specific date. If not, try to get it advanced so it will meet the payment terms.

Customer Contact Methods

The most effective method of customer contact is made via telephone, which can elicit a timely or, it is hoped, immediate response. Once you have the proper person on the phone, you are well positioned to secure a commitment to pay or determine the reason for nonpayment. In our experience, e-mail is a very effective method of communicating with accounts payable departments. Many people respond more promptly to e-mails than voice mails, and the e-mail message is much better at conveying invoice numbers, amounts due, and so on.

Collection letters have limited effectiveness. They are best used with low-priority, small-balance accounts that probably will not receive a call or personalized e-mail. For such accounts, a collection letter is better than no contact at all. A small percentage of letters do elicit a payment or report of a dispute. Collection letters also help when escalating action with a delinquent customer. Strong action is appropriate when it follows repeated collection contacts that were ignored. It is easier to justify holding orders when you can cite prior collection letters and calls to the customer.

In the final analysis, the justification of collection letters is that they are better than nothing. With praise like this, who needs criticism? Since collection letters are of low value, they must be automated to ensure that the time and cost expended on them is minimal. An experienced, very successful director of customer financial services at a $2 billion test equipment manufacturer says that he has never seen truly automated collection letters. They always involve some manual processing. Truly automated means:

- The system selects customers to receive a letter, excluding customers coded to be exempt from collection letters (typically, the larger accounts, which receive calls), by reading the delinquency status and excluding disputed items (and late payment fees and unearned discounts if desired).

- The system selects the appropriate letter based on the degree of delinquency. (The more past due an invoice, the more urgent tone in the letter.)

- The system prints the letter with an itemized list of delinquent invoices and other charges and credits. Letters should be phrased in a customer service–oriented manner, but call for prompt, specific, action: for example, "pay $8756.29 by July 17." The letters should prominently display the payment address and specifics for electronic and procurement card payments, as well as a person's name and number to call (usually the assigned collector). Company letterhead should be used.

- The system prints the envelopes.

- There is no human review of the letters. They are simply inserted in the envelopes and mailed promptly.

- Collection letters are best delivered via e-mail for greater speed and cost efficiency.

- Collection letters should be run at least twice per month to avoid triggering a huge volume of incoming calls, which can paralyze collection staff members and divert them from focusing on the large dollar amounts. This is especially true when there is a lot of clutter in the receivables portfolio.

Statements of account are similar to collection letters with these differences:

- They show all open items on a customer account, not just the delinquent ones.

- They should be sent to all customers every month. Part of the mission of receivables management is to help customers maintain their credit accounts with you in the best possible condition. Clearing open items, especially clutter items, is an important part of the service provided your customer. Statements display all open items, enable customers to see the entire account, and enable them to apply open credits or payments to open debits. Statements can also save the customer and you a great deal of

▶ CASE HISTORY ◀

Mailing All Statements at Once Creates Unmanageable Volume of Incoming Calls

An apparel manufacturer with over 10,000 customers had very inaccurate cash application. As a result, most of its customer statements of account were inaccurate, with many displaying the remaining amounts of misapplied customer payments. The manufacturer mailed 10,000 customer statements in a single batch every month. The volume of incoming calls that resulted overwhelmed the collection and customer service staff. Most of the calls were from very small balance customers, and many were to request a refund of the open credit transactions on the account. The incoming calls consumed all of the collection staff's time, so that virtually no outbound collection calls were made for several months. Cash flow decreased severely.

work if their account is selected for verification as part of an audit. Sending statements every month also helps justify escalation when needed.

- The comments about collection letters concerning automation, delivering a collection message, providing remittance information, and delivering via e-mail, apply to statements as well.

Customer visits are a valuable tool in developing and reinforcing a positive rapport with the customer. They should be utilized subject to expense constraints, as they are time consuming and can involve travel expense. However, visits are entirely appropriate for large and/or problem accounts.

Customer visits have two objectives:

1. To introduce or reinforce a business relationship between a collector and the customer's accounts payable person
2. To discuss the status of the customer's account and clearance of open items

Two tools can be used for this purpose:

1. A reconciliation pack of the customer's account (explained later in this section)
2. An end-of-month account statement

In all cases, the document must be sent well in advance so the customer can prepare a response. In addition, you must be make it clear to the customer that you expect the research to be completed before the meeting, so the meeting will focus on resolution and clearing of the open items.

Customer visits should be conducted by the collector, accompanied by the sales representative. An invitation should be extended to the collection manager as well.

Preparation for the visit should include thorough review of these materials:

- The reconciliation pack or statement sent to the customer along with all supporting documentation. Items that have cleared should be identified the day before the meeting to save time during the meeting.

- An up-to-date statement of account.

- A perspective of the customer's prevailing payment habits (quantified if possible).

- A list of key people in the accounts payable department with their phone numbers.

- Authorization of bargaining power to concede items when necessary.

The meeting itself should focus on agreeing how to clear open transactions on the customer's account, whether via payment or adjustment.

After the meeting, the collector should send an e-mail or letter thanking the customer for his or her time and summarizing the actions agreed to by both parties. Then the actions should be initiated as soon as possible to reinforce credibility with the customer.

Preparation for Customer Contact

Best Practice preparation for a call or e-mail involves the following steps:

1. Select a customer to contact based on the prioritization methodology (next largest open amount or high risk).

2. Retrieve the contact name and phone number from your receivables system.

3. Call up that customer's current account status on the receivables system.

4. Review the status summarizing the total amount due in each aging category, so you can state the amount past due and amount falling due in your opening remarks.

5. Review the notes of prior conversations in the system to refresh your memory on recent conversations.

6. Review the last reconciliation pack sent if applicable.

7. Note any clutter transactions (unapplied cash, short payments) you intend to discuss with the customer.

8. Quickly formulate the request you will make of the customer, and assemble supporting documents. Display the customer's account on the computer screen.

9. You are now ready to make the call (or e-mail).

For the preparation of a contact for collecting short-paid invoices:

1. Identify any unapplied cash, credit memos, or adjustments that you believe may apply to the open transactions so you can secure the customer's approval to apply.

2. Review the notes of your last discussion of these items and/or any return correspondence.

3. Assemble supporting documentation.

4. Make the call (or e-mail).

Execution of the Customer Contact

To reiterate, customer contact can be made by phone, e-mail, or fax. The preferred method is by telephone; however, customers' preference for e-mail or fax, if they respond to it in a timely manner, is acceptable.

It is essential that collection contact be made with a person at the customer who can produce the desired effect—that is, pay the invoices and provide information as to their status. The first contact is usually with the accounts payable department.

The communication should begin by identifying yourself by name, "of the customer financial services or credit or collection department." You should then inform the contact of the reason for the call, stating the status of account according to your records, confirming that their records agree with the past due invoices, and asking when the invoices will be paid.

A suggested script (to be modified to fit your own style) is:

"Hello, this is　　[name]　　of　　[company name]　　calling to discuss the status of your account. Our records show you have　　xxx　　dollars past due and　　xxx　　dollars falling due in the next few days. Do your records agree?"

If not, pinpoint the discrepancy to determine if the customer is missing invoices, disputing invoices, or have deductions to be taken. It may be helpful to send a copy of a statement of account to facilitate the discussion. If a customer is missing invoices, provide the customer with a copy.

If invoices are disputed, get complete information about the nature of the dispute so you can initiate its resolution. If there is a disagreement as to the due date of the invoices, carefully explain the payment terms and the due dates. If necessary, provide documentation (contract) to support the agreed payment terms and their interpretation.

The objective is to get the customer to include *all* invoices that are past due and falling due in the next payment. (This is known as total inclusion.) The amount paid may be less than the sum of all the invoices because of deductions, but ensure all invoices are paid.

If the customer agrees with the amount and due dates, secure a commitment as to the date, amount, and invoices to be paid.

Upon completion of the call, take these five steps:

1. Enter into the collection notes the results of the contact, including: payment date, amount, check number if available, and a description of invoices to be paid (e.g., "all May invoices"). Enter your initials, the date, and the name of the person(s) to whom you spoke. Utilization of standard abbreviations can accelerate this process.

2. Enter into your diary follow-up mechanism the date of the next action (e.g., follow-up on payment promise).

3. If appropriate, confirm the agreed actions in writing or e-mail.

4. Fulfill actions you have promised within 48 hours.

5. Initiate resolution actions for any disputes you have identified within 48 hours.

If you cannot get through and you get voice mail:

- Try calling back two or three times before leaving a message.
- Make follow-up e-mails and faxes after two days if no response received.

Negotiation Skills and Empowerment

Best Practices includes empowering collectors to negotiate and to concede charges during negotiation. Limits must be placed on the amount that can be conceded. Concessions can also be limited to late payment fees and unearned prompt payment discounts. However, to achieve best results *most efficiently*, a collector must be empowered to write off certain amounts. This empowers collectors with the customer and eliminates the time required to secure approvals.

Negotiation plays an important role in collections. However, it is not the classic, pure negotiation that transpires between a willing buyer and willing seller. It is different because:

- The deal has already been agreed.
- The customer has implicitly agreed to the payment terms. You are merely asking the customer to abide by what has already been agreed.

However, the customer's ability or willingness to pay may be limited, and that is when negotiation enters the process.

The seven key steps in collection negotiations are:

1. Prepare by reviewing the status of the account, prior actions and discussions, and what you wish to achieve.
2. Decide what you will concede.
3. State your opening position; for example, "We expect all invoices to be paid by the due date."

4. If the customer does not commit to the opening position, propose an alternative, and look for a willingness to bargain.

5. Bargain using proposals and counter proposals in an "if, then" format. Trade items of low value to you that may be of high value to the customer. Examples: grant a little more time to pay in return for releasing orders, paying late payment fees, and so on.

6. Agree to all conditions.

7. Confirm in writing afterward.

Payment Plans

Payment plans should be negotiated only when the customer cannot pay all the past due amount within a 30-day time frame. The objectives in negotiating a payment plan are:

- Payments should be of the shortest duration possible.
- Plans should include a high frequency of payments.
- Plan should begin with an immediate payment of a significant amount.
- Secure postdated checks for future payments.
- Include a finance charge for extending the time period for full payment.

Collections staff members should discuss all impending negotiations for payment plans in advance with the collection manager, whenever possible, to agree with the parameters of the payment plan. Once negotiations begin, the collector must be empowered to unilaterally reach an agreement within the agreed parameters with the customer.

All payment plans must be confirmed in writing. In instances where the amount is large and/or the time period extended beyond six months, a promissory note and/or other security instrument should be executed. Payment dates must be entered into the collector's diary follow-up mechanism and followed up with a proactive contact before each payment date.

Dealing with Problem Customers

Problem customers are customers that are chronically slow in paying and/or pose a high level of risk of nonpayment. In addition to the cost of funding the slow payments and the risk of bad debt loss, problem customers inflict a high cost in servicing their accounts. This cost is reflected in increased collector time, but also in the time of credit, finance, sales, and executive management. Imany, Inc., a collection software firm, estimates that problem accounts require four to five times as much time to manage as nonproblem accounts.[1] Given the high actual and potential cost of these accounts, how are they best handled?

The best way is to do business with them differently. Instead of selling on open account and then chasing them for past due receivables, sell them on a more restricted basis, such as:

- Lower credit limit with immediate order hold when the limit is exceeded or a delinquency threshold is violated
- Shorter payment terms
- Up-front deposit
- Direct debit of their bank account on the invoice due date
- Standby letter of credit
- Cash with order
- Other security devices (guarantees, etc.)

Implementing any of these terms may result in lower sales to problem accounts. This risk of lower profit earned on the sales must be weighed against the cost, management time, and risk of bad debt loss of the existing mode of business, and is best made by executive management.

Payment plans (see above) are useful for reining in a seriously delinquent problem customer.

Another useful technique is called "burning the candle at both ends." Typically, when working with a problem customer, the focus is on securing payment for the oldest past due invoices first, then working on the remaining invoices in order of greatest age. Unfortunately, as the oldest invoices are being paid over a period of time, ongoing shipments begin to age and quickly become past due. The first rule in dealing with problem accounts is that the amount of payments must exceed the level of sales, to ensure the total balance is continuously decreasing. The "burning the candle at both ends" technique involves securing payment for the old invoices, while simultaneously securing payment for some current invoices. This will reduce the amount of future past due debt to be dealt with. This technique may not always result in an absolute greater amount of payments, but often it can. Additionally, it continues the urgency caused by seriously past due invoices, while decreasing the total exposure.

Finally, the escalation protocol (or collection timeline) prescribes the actions to be taken for a seriously delinquent customer. When the above-mentioned techniques fail, the escalation protocol must be followed. In our experience, many companies hope and wish for improvement with problem customers, but in most cases, the exposure increases as time advances. Delaying order and shipment hold usually results in higher exposure and a bigger problem. If substantial improvement is not seen, and commitments for short-term payments are not secured, it is best to face facts and refer the account to a collection agency or attorney. These third parties are most effective the earlier they take over an account. For a number of reasons (credit reporting, experience), they can exert pressure and achieve results that the supplier company cannot. It is far better to collect a significant portion of a problem account's receivable and pay the commission to a third party than to procrastinate, hoping against the odds, and end up with a large loss. The suppliers that utilize third parties first usually achieve the best results. If you are the tenth supplier to refer an account to a collection agency, it has little impact. If you are the first or second, your chances of collection are much better. The best way to ensure that the collectors are using the Best Practices is through two primary actions:

1. Have the supervisor sit with each collector for two to three hours while the collector is making collection calls. The preparation, execution, and post-call follow-up can be observed and constructive suggestions for improvement offered.

2. Have the supervisor conduct periodic (weekly is best) portfolio reviews with each collector. The portfolio review is a review of the status and next steps to be taken with a group of accounts. Usually the accounts selected are the larger ones or the problem accounts. It is also a good practice to select some medium and smaller accounts to test how well the portfolio is being penetrated. The portfolio reviews will enable the supervisor to obtain a perspective on how well collectors move accounts to a satisfactory condition, if their follow-up intervals are too long, how well they are pushing coworkers to resolve issues, and so on.

Key Points

The six key points to remember about the collection process are:

1. It is a process and it must be well defined. The collection timeline helps in the definition and in communicating and explaining it within your organization.

2. It must be supported throughout the organization, not just by finance.

3. It is designed to execute the portfolio strategy and, as a result, should be tailored to the major segments of the portfolio.

4. Weekly portfolio reviews are essential to achieving top performance from collectors.

5. Proven fundamentals apply to virtually all portfolio segments.

6. More customer contact is better than less. Earlier contact is better than later.

National Accounts Approach

A national account is defined as a large, important customer that provides a significant portion of total sales and profit. Typically they are large Fortune 1000–size companies, with multiple locations (or ship-to addresses), and a contract governing the trading. Often they are very creditworthy. Losing such a customer would be a serious adverse event for a company. The objective of receivables management for national accounts is to provide premium financial service to them and to maximize cash flow from them.

In an effort to retain and grow revenue with such customers, companies will provide a premium level of service. Premium service can take many forms, but in revenue cycle operations, it often includes some or all of these areas:

- Staff members dedicated to the contract and pricing administration, order processing, and in some cases invoicing and payment processing of a national accounts customer(s). This enables the staff members to specialize in the needs and procedures of the customer(s) and develop a rapport with their counterparts within the customer. Specialized staff members are often used for government customers that have particular and inflexible contracting and invoicing requirements. Order fulfillment, invoicing accuracy, and dispute resolution are enhanced by specialized staff members.

- Enhanced service standards, usually faster turnaround times for order processing and dispute resolution.

- Dedicated collectors who utilize a "national accounts" approach to the appropriate customers. Such an approach is designed to recognize the unique characteristics and value of national account customers. The approach includes:

    - Account maintenance focusing on skipped invoices (providing invoice copies, proof of delivery, etc.), deduction and dis-

► CASE HISTORY ◄

Superior Service for National Account

A telecommunications company instituted a two-hour turnaround standard for all orders for a large national account. Specific customer service staff members were designated to handle this customer's orders. Backup staff members were also designated and a supervisor assigned to allocate workloads to ensure the standard was met.

pute clearing, application of open credit memos and payments, and the overall clearing of clutter.

- Customer service–based "collection" calls for skipped invoices. Such "calls" are often e-mail messages.
- Prompt deduction and dispute resolution.
- Periodic customer visits to build rapport.
- Use of credit hold only in extreme cases that have been escalated to senior management of both companies.
- Construction of "payer profiles" that document the approval and payment process of the customer and information on key contacts in procurement, accounts payable, and finance.

Successful national account administration enables companies to manage large revenue streams and receivable assets with excellent results. Conversely, mismanagement of national accounts administration can result in receivables nightmares that can be disproportionate to the size of the customer. Exhibit 3.7 illustrates how a national account that comprised 16% of a firm's revenue and was poorly administered soon accounted for the lion's share of receivables problems.

SPECIAL COLLECTION EFFORTS

Overview

Special collection efforts are initiatives focused on narrowly defined objectives. Excellent management of the receivables asset is a broad objective. Two common examples of narrowly defined objectives are:

1. Reducing the value and number of seriously aged open items
2. Maximizing cash collections over the next 120 days

Special collection efforts focus additional resource and management time on their objectives. By concentrating resources and attention on a limited task, progress can be accelerated and results improved. Other tasks and duties can be deferred or delayed, while maximum resources

Exhibit 3.7 National Account Impact

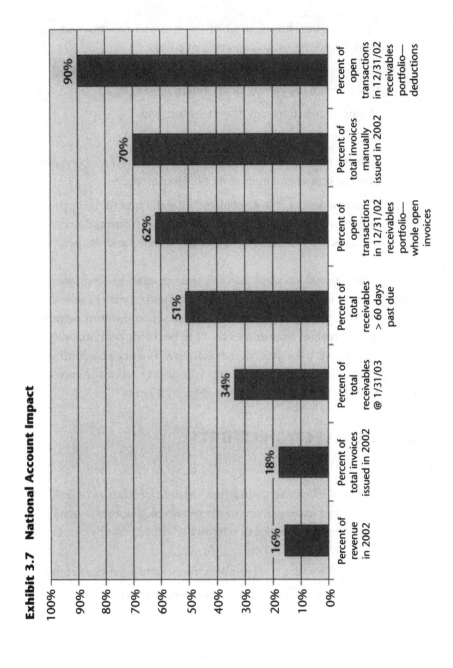

are devoted to the special efforts. Alternatively, additional resources can be deployed to maintain activity levels in all areas.

Often, special efforts are initiated to solve problems that have built up over a long period of time and are not being resolved satisfactorily in the normal course of business.

Two special collection efforts directed at common receivables management problems are described next.

Best Practices

Reconciliation and Recovery

This effort (or program) is directed at substantially reducing the value and number of aged open items. Often these aged items are defined as 90 to 120 days old, and can be found in the far right column of the receivables aging report. These receivables are at the greatest risk of bad debt loss, usually trigger a high level of provisioning in the bad debt reserve, and draw a lot of senior management and auditor attention. These items pose a difficult dilemma:

If they were easily cleared, it would have been done before they reached the advanced age. It will take much time, effort, and cost to try to collect and clear them. However, their collectability is low, especially if there are many clutter transactions included. So companies are faced with the prospect of expending a great deal of resources for a relatively small payback. On the other hand, to just write them off is too costly. If the collection staff is assigned to devote a substantial portion of its time to work these accounts, cash flow will decrease as the normal collection effort will be diminished. How can this dilemma be solved?

The answer is a reconciliation and recovery program. A reconciliation and recovery program:

- Identifies customer accounts with a large number of aged, clutter transactions. Customers with less than eight such transactions and customers with just whole open invoices are excluded from the program. Such accounts can be handled by the collectors in the normal course of collections without consuming too much of their time.

- Defines a format for presenting your claim and its supporting documentation to the customer. The format is called a reconciliation pack, and contains these elements:
  - A customer service–oriented cover letter stating that this is a recap of the aged items open on your records, asking them to review and prepare a response
  - A summary of all aged open items by transaction types (i.e., invoice, short payments, credit memos, unapplied payments, etc.)
  - A detailed listing of all open transactions with transaction number, date, and original and remaining amounts
  - Copies of invoices, credit memos, etc.
  - Copies of proofs of delivery (POD) if necessary. Sometimes it is more time efficient to exclude them for all open invoices and await the customer's request for the missing ones.
- Utilizes high-speed procedures with decision points for assembling the packs. These procedures are developed by an expert on staff who can document the fastest, most efficient method of assembly. Decision points are used to maintain the cost efficiency focus. An example of a decision point is if a copy of a one-year-old invoice for a small dollar amount cannot be retrieved, then it is best to write it off rather than expend inordinate amounts of time searching. Similarly, small clutter items may be unilaterally written off to reduce the time and expense of reconciliation pack assembly.
- Utilizes temporarily assigned clerical workers to assemble the reconciliation packs. This saves collectors an enormous amount of time, allowing them to focus on collections. Assembly of the packs requires customer accounting and document retrieval skills, which are less costly than collection skills. In addition, when the program is finished, the resources can be discontinued.
- Utilizes the collector as the person to discuss the pack with the customer and drive collection and clearing of all the aged open items. This is often accomplished with a face-to-face meeting.

The organization of a reconciliation and recovery program should follow these seven steps:

1. Compile the list of customer accounts for which a reconciliation pack is to be prepared.

2. Document the contents and format of a reconciliation pack and the high-speed procedures for assembling it.

3. Estimate the time required for retrieval for each type of transaction (e.g., invoice, credit memo, unapplied payment, etc.) and for the assembly of the pack. Estimate the time required to assemble a pack for each customer on the list.

4. Calculate the number of clerical staff required to assemble all the packs in the desired time frame. It is always wise to plan on more staff, especially if temporary workers are used to insulate against their frequent turnover.

5. Assemble and train the reconciliation team, and designate a supervisor who will answer questions and drive results. An internal staff member is a good choice here, as his or her familiarity with the company and its systems will be valuable in guiding the temporary staff.

6. Assign and schedule the completion of the packs among the reconciliation staff.

7. Track the progress of the program on a weekly basis, noting specifically:

   a. The actual completion of packs versus the schedule

   b. The actual follow-up of the packs with the customer by the collectors

   c. The progress in clearing the aged items, differentiating between cash and noncash (adjustments, write-offs) reasons for clearing

Remember, the ultimate objective is to clear the aged items, maximizing cash recovery, but within the time and cost guidelines established. Some companies are reluctant to write off even small amounts, resulting in prolonging the program and its cost.

The measurement of the program can be tricky. The best way is to "freeze" the aged items in the program. Every day additional items will age over into the 90- to 120-day column. However, unless you disregard these items, program progress will be obscured. By limiting the

---

▶ CASE HISTORY ◀

Three Reconciliation and Recovery Program Success Stories

Case One
A distributor of laboratory supplies had accumulated $48 million of receivables over 150 days past due as a result of acquisition integration issues. These receivables were spread over 25,000 different customers and were comprised of over 150,000 items (many of which were clutter). Implementation of a reconciliation and recovery program reduced this portfolio of aged receivables to $3 million in eight months, with open items decreasing to under 5,000. The cash recovery rate was 71%, which was much better than the company had reserved for.

Case Two
A test equipment manufacturer had accumulated over $6 million of receivables over 180 days past due as a result of a difficult ERP implementation. These receivables were comprised of almost 18,000 open items, many of which were clutter transactions. They were spread over 1,000 customers, and many were over two years old. The company implemented a reconciliation and recovery program with a team of six staff. In six months, over $4 million of the aged receivables were cleared, with 64% being collected in cash. The number of open items was reduced by 68%.

Case Three
A high-transaction-volume distributor had accumulated $1.6 million of over 90 days past due receivables, comprised of over 8,000 open items spread over 175 customer accounts. Implementation of a recovery and reconciliation program cleared half of the aged receivables in four months with a 90% cash recovery.

transactions in the program to a fixed, finite set, you can accurately track the progress in clearing these items.

This progress can be measured by defining the aged items on the target list as all items over xx days old as of a specific date.

These examples illustrate how effective a reconciliation and recovery program can be. Two important points are:

1. The inclusion of less aged items increases the cash recovery. As long as you are preparing a reconciliation pack, it requires little incremental effort to include items as little as 90 days past due. However, inclusion of too many items will cause the pack to be too daunting a task for the customer.

2. These programs take months, not weeks. Increasing resources can accelerate the completion of the packs, but time is needed to organize the effort, recruit and train staff, and so on. Also, the clearing depends a great deal on the timing of the customer response, and it is unreasonable to expect a response to a pack in less than two weeks.

High-Impact Action Program

A proven technique for maximizing cash collections in the short term is called a high-impact action program. The basic premise of a high-impact action program is to implement only those actions that:

- Can be developed and implemented within one month
- Will yield results in two to three months

This eliminates some important initiatives, such as automation, formal dispute management, major redesign of processes, and so on, which can be addressed in a longer-term program.

The objectives of a high-impact action program are to:

- Increase cash receipts as much as possible as soon as possible
- Clean up the portfolio (uncollectibles, offsets, etc.) to produce a smaller, less complex asset to manage in the future

A high-impact action program starts with a one- to two-week planning stage. Typically, such a program includes these seven elements:

1. Categorize the receivables portfolio into segments based on customer attributes (size, domestic vs. foreign, national account or not, government vs. private sector, line of business, reseller/partner or end user, etc.), or billing status (billed vs. unbilled) that require a specialized approach.

2. Develop and document high-speed procedures for each specialized approach (e.g., call blitz, collection letters, reconciliation packs, etc.).

3. Develop and implement a collection infrastructure (negotiation empowerment, escalation protocol, ad hoc dispute process, document retrieval, credit controls, etc.).

4. Design the organization to execute the high-impact action program utilizing existing staff, with supplements if necessary, especially for administrative and/or reconciliation support. Train staff in high-speed procedures, provide workspace, tools, and so on.

▶ **CASE HISTORY** ◀

Three Examples of High-Impact Action Progams Getting High-Impact Results

Case One
A leading software developer had seen its cash collections deteriorate over time because of significant systems and organization changes. In an attempt to recover the shortfall in cash flow and increase cash collections in the short term, the company implemented a High-Impact Action Program. It supplemented its collection staff members and dedicated them to the High-Impact Action Program, suspending activity on all other initiatives. It developed and implemented an ad hoc dispute resolution process, secured senior management buy-in, and launched the program. In its first full quarter of

Case History *(continued)*

operation, it increased cash collections by 22% (over $20 million) over the preceding quarter, on equivalent revenue. It also cleared via adjustment, credit memo, or write-off another $7 million of receivables. This jump-started an initiative to improve receivable management results, which, over a two-year period, reduced DSO by over 40% and increased cash reserves by over 25%.

Case Two
An equipment vendor needed cash for an impending debt repayment. It decided to raise the cash from its receivables asset, instead of seeking alternate borrowing. It launched a High-Impact Action Program by assembling a supplemental group of collectors who would take over approximately one-third of each permanent collector's portfolio. This would enable the permanent collectors to devote more time and effort to their remaining accounts, with the net result of all accounts receiving substantially more intense attention. The results were striking. In only two months, overall delinquency decreased by 43%. Amounts between 30 and 90 days past due were reduced an astonishing 81%. Not surprisingly, the past dues over 90 days past due were decreased only 23%, revealing the more difficult nature of seriously past due receivables. This is the exact reason why a Reconciliation and Recovery Program is needed for such receivables.

Case Three
A fast-growing manufacturer of therapy devices was experiencing disappointing cash collections. The rate of increase in collections was well below the growth rate of revenue. To correct this problem in the short term, the company launched a High-Impact Action Program. It supplemented the collectors with temporary administrative help and ensured that customer service incoming calls were routed to the customer service department. This allowed the collectors to focus on collection activity. It reallocated customer accounts more evenly to ensure better portfolio penetration, conducted refresher collection training, and measured progress toward targets on a daily basis. The results were a 33% increase in cash collections in only three months of operation. Cash collection records for a day, week, and month were set.

5. Implement the collection activity plan to monitor and measure progress. This tool is explained later in the book, but it measures activities (inputs) as well as results (outputs).

6. Secure management approval, announce to the organization, then launch the program.

7. Manage the program with experienced, tactical, hands-on supervision, and *drive results*.

Key Points

The five key points to remember about high-impact action programs are:

1. Focus resource and management attention. Divert or suspend other tasks.

2. Secure senior management support.

3. Raise activity levels. (Supplemental resources are very helpful.)

4. Measure both activities and results vs. stretch targets on a daily or weekly basis.

5. Seriously aged receivables and/or clutter are best handled by a reconciliation and recovery program.

DEDUCTIONS PROCESSING

Overview

A deduction occurs when a customer pays an invoice less than the full amount. Deductions are also called short payments. Customers take deductions when they do not agree with the amount of the invoice or if they believe they are owed money by the vendor. Instead of waiting for the vendor to issue a credit memo, which would be applied to their next remittance, companies take the deduction because it puts money in their pocket now rather than waiting weeks for the credit memo. Some customers may withhold payment of the entire invoice until it is resolved to their satisfaction (via a corrected invoice or credit memo), but most will deduct.

Examples of disagreements with the invoice are:

- Price: gross, promotional, discount
- Quantity of products or service hours received
- Quality: damaged or inferior products or services

Examples of deductions taken because the customer is owed money by the vendor:

- Volume or other rebates
- Cooperative advertising support
- Return of products not yet credited (We have seen cases where the returns were not shipped, yet the deduction was still taken.)
- Shelf space charges
- Charges for special handling of mislabeled or poorly packaged products, or products delivered to the wrong location

Customers, especially large retailers, have become very creative and very aggressive with deductions. Deductions are taken unilaterally by customers, based on their perception of whether the invoice was correct, the shipment proper, and so on. Even if a vendor conformed to all customer specifications and invoiced 100% accurately, it would still incur deductions.

For many companies, the volume of deductions taken by their customers can number in the thousands every month. Unless such companies have an efficient process for handling deductions, they will be overwhelmed by the volume. There are two major perils of not processing deductions well or on a timely basis:

1. Revenue and profit margins will decrease because of invalid deductions taken by customers.

2. Revenue and receivables will be overstated in financial reports. This is critically important with the passage of the Sarbanes-Oxley Act of 2002.

The three dilemmas in managing deductions are:

1. The volumes can be huge, and the damage can be serious if they are not managed well.
2. The cost of processing and managing deductions can be substantial.
3. The yield or payback can be small. Typically, customers are correct on approximately 95% of the deductions they take. It is not cost efficient to expend a large amount of resources and expense to scrutinize every deduction, when 95% of them will be conceded. If you do nothing, however, some customers will become more aggressive in taking deductions, and margins will suffer.

The challenge is to process deductions promptly so they do not distort financial reporting, to catch and recover invalid ones, and not to spend a lot of money to process adjustments 95% of the time. It is a daunting challenge, and the resolution must balance the cost/benefit trade-off in a way that fits an individual company's strategy and profitability.

Best Practices

Deduction processing is a science in and of itself, and a book could be devoted entirely to this subject. Many types of deductions, their cause, and resolution, are industry specific. We cannot address industry-specific issues, but will deal with a broader perspective of Best Practices. The optimal deduction process must be tailored to an individual company, its products or services, its profit margins, and its market power and that of its customers.

The best way to handle deductions is to reduce the number incurred. This is much easier said than done, especially when the customer is in

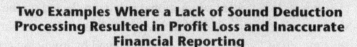

CASE HISTORY

Two Examples Where a Lack of Sound Deduction Processing Resulted in Profit Loss and Inaccurate Financial Reporting

Case One

A food products manufacturer, selling to major retailers, lacked an efficient and effective deduction process. Staff members were overwhelmed with the thousands of deductions incurred each month and fell way behind in clearing deductions. There were a number of negative impacts:

- Customers were getting away with invalid deductions as they were not challenged promptly or properly.
- Deductions constituted over half of the total receivables; many were aged over six months to a year.
- Revenue, profit, and receivables were overstated in the financial reports.

Case Two

In another case, a distributor had no formal process for deductions. It did have a policy that all open items over 180 days past due were to be written off. As a result, deductions would be untouched for 180 days, at which point they were written off. The company was losing an unknown amount of profit from invalid customer deductions. This $350 million company later discovered that invalid deductions totaled over $500,000 per year.

a superior position—that is, when there are several suppliers of your product, and the customer does not have to change its mode of business to suit any individual vendor's request. This is the most common situation.

However, two actions can be taken unilaterally to reduce the number of deductions taken by your customers. These are:

1. Ensuring orders are fulfilled, packaged, documented (packing slip, etc.), labeled (bar code), and shipped in accordance with customer specifications. This will preempt special handling deductions.

2. Ensuring invoice accuracy, reflecting the accurate net or discounted price agreed with the customer. Unfortunately, many customers do not want promotional pricing reflected on the invoice, preferring to take it "off invoice." This preference limits the amount of deduction reduction achieved by invoicing accuracy. However, there usually are some invoicing errors that, if prevented, can reduce deductions.

There are also two actions that can be negotiated with customers to reduce deductions:

1. An allowance for damage, shortages, and so on can be negotiated to cover expected losses for this type of event. Typically, the allowance is expressed as a percentage of the price and is based on historical experience. The allowance percent can be granted on every invoice or taken on a quarterly basis. In return, the customer agrees to refrain from taking deductions for the specified reasons. This can have a huge impact on decreasing the volume of incoming deductions.

2. Agreement to settle some obligations owed the customer with a payables wire transfer or check. Examples of such obligations are lump-sum promotional support for advertising, shelf space, slotting, and so on. The best expenses for this type of arrangement are low-frequency charges.

Finally, abuse of deductions by a customer (i.e., taking a high volume of invalid deductions) has to be addressed. It is best addressed by senior management of both companies agreeing to the parameters of a business relationship/partnership. Receivables clerks cannot change the behavior of large customers.

Efforts to reduce incoming deductions generally produce a significant payback and are the best way to deal with deductions.

Deductions Processing

As stated earlier, optimal deduction processing must be significantly tailored to an individual company's business. However, 12 common techniques are essential to efficient, effective deduction processing. They are:

1. Small-balance automatic write-off in cash application. "Automatic" means that there is no investigation of their validity, they are just written off. Best Practice is for the small-balance deductions to be cleared by the system tool, clearing the open item and charging the appropriate ledger account. In our experience, small deductions often comprise 30 to 40% of the deductions, but only 2 to 5% of the value. An enormous amount of work can be saved while sacrificing an opportunity to reclaim a very small amount of money. Remember, less than 5% of deductions are ever recovered, so 5% of a small value is a very small opportunity.

   We have worked with companies whose small-balance write-off threshold has ranged from $25 to $400. The way to establish the threshold is to compare the cost of researching a deduction against the expected return of the effort. Small-balance thresholds can vary based on the type of deduction. We elaborate on this below.

   Finally, audit and sample check write-offs retrospectively to identify abusive customers and recurring amounts that may indicate a continuing billing/price dispute. Some customers test their suppliers' threshold and will frequently deduct an amount just below the perceived threshold. Repeat offenders can be discovered with the retrospective audit. Alternatively, you may be invoicing a customer the wrong price on a high-volume item shipped in the same quantity numerous times, and that customer may be continually deducting the same amount.

2. Clear communication of instructions to customers as to where to send information on deductions (i.e., debit memos). Some customers post information on the Web (e.g., Fleming Foods' Vision Net), so vendors can ascertain the reason for an individual deduction referencing the vendor's transaction number.

3. Classification of deductions by type at point of entry (cash application). This has three benefits:

a. It enables processing and the small-balance automatic write-off to be varied by the type of deduction based on probability of collection.

b. It enables routing of deductions to the person or department within the company best positioned to resolve them quickly and properly.

c. It enables root cause analysis of high-frequency deductions. Such analysis guides internal continuous improvement efforts to improve order fulfillment, invoicing, and so on to reduce the number of incoming deductions.

4. Establishment of standard time frames for resolution of deductions. Speed is critically important for recovery of invalid deductions and for overall process efficiency. Staff and departments outside the deductions processing unit must understand the deadline for resolving deductions assigned to them.

5. Documentation, communication, and training in a clear deductions process, work flows, research methodology, and roles and responsibilities. Exhibit 3.8 is an illustrative diagram of a deduction process and work flow.

6. Utilization of a deduction prioritization methodology. This methodology does not treat all deductions the same. It prioritizes them for research and resolution based on their probability of collection (if found to be invalid). To illustrate this point, consider two different types of deductions: a deduction for a "concealed" quantity shortage and a deduction for using the same credit memo twice. It is almost impossible to prove a customer is wrong about a concealed shortage (a shortage where the standard package contains, say, 24 items and the customer claims to have received only 21). On the other hand, if the customer used the same credit memo twice, that is easy to prove, and the probability of collecting the invalid deduction is very high. To achieve maximum recoveries at peak efficiency, the effort of a deduction team should be focused on those types of deductions that have a high probability of collection.

Exhibit 3.8 Deduction Processing Workflow

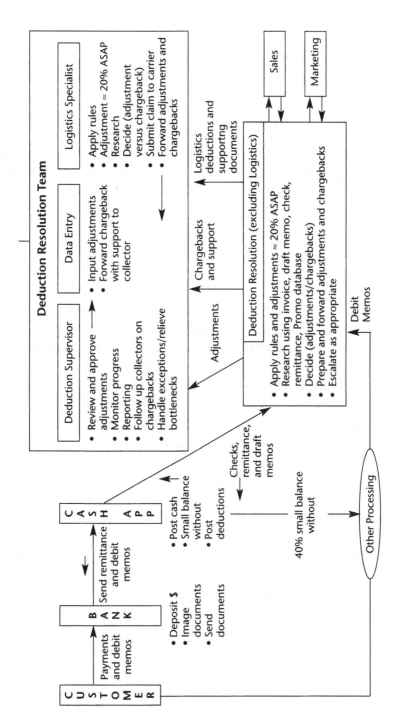

99

A deduction prioritization methodology utilizes a different small-balance write-off threshold for different types of deductions. High-probability-of-collection deduction types have a relatively low threshold, and low-probability-of-collection deduction types have a high threshold. Remember, you want to match the level of effort with the expected payback. Why expend a lot of time researching a deduction if you will be unable to recover it even if it is found to be invalid?

7. Provision of accurate, up-to-date information on sales promotions offered customers. This is best accomplished by establishing and populating a promotions database. Commercial software applications exist to automate this function and make it widely available through a company's intranet, server, and/or on the Web, so all constituents can access it. This information must include a description and quantification of the promotion, effective dates, eligible customers, and a clear explanation on how it is applied and earned by the customer. Only properly authorized promotions should be included in the promotions database. Promotions must be loaded in the database *prior* to their effective date.

The advantage of a promotions database is the efficiency it brings to the research and resolution of deductions. Remember that 95% (or more) of deductions are allowed. If a customer properly takes a deduction for an authorized deduction, it should be allowed. If the staff member researching the deduction can easily and quickly determine it was a proper deduction, then the adjustment (or credit memo) can be promptly issued, matched to the open deduction, and cleared from the ledger. This is where efficiency is realized.

8. Measurement and reporting of key metrics such as:

   a. Throughput (deductions received and cleared in a period)

   b. Average cycle time to clear deductions

   c. Backlog of deductions(quantity and age)

    d. Ultimate outcome (adjusted or charged back, and percent of chargebacks actually collected)

9. Utilization of technology (system tools) to automate work flow and tasks. A number of commercial applications on the market automate much of the deductions process. Most of them are combined with credit and/or collection applications as well. In addition, major ERP systems have deduction processing capability. Leveraging technology is critical to achieving efficiency in this high-transaction volume function. Imaging of documents with Web access is also important, so all members of your firm can access data and documents wherever they are. In some cases, it is advantageous to grant customers, brokers, and/or agents access to this data, especially when you are enlisting their aid to resolve deductions.

10. Development of a fast, efficient returns processing capability. (This applies only to companies with tangible products.) Returns are often the leading cause of deductions, and those deductions are of the highest value. The ability to receive and inspect returns and to issue the appropriate credit or chargeback is essential to excellence in deduction processing. Bar coding and scanning technology in conjunction with a return authorization procedure will help process authorized returns quickly. Unfortunately, many customers will return products without an authorization number, which requires exception handling.

11. Customer profitability analysis of major customers, which includes the impact of deductions on profitability. Also, the major deduction types as a percent of sales for each major customer should be measured to enable comparison. This enables identification of high-deduction customers. Corrective action can be taken to improve order fulfillment quality and direct senior management action with the customer as needed. For example, assume the overall average for returns is 1.2% of sales, but one major customer is returning 4.5% of sales. Two actions should be taken:

a. A review of internal order fulfillment for that customer to ensure orders are being filled properly and to customer specifications

b. If order fulfillment is satisfactory, a discussion with the customer to identify the excessive rate of returns and to formulate ways to reduce it

The measurement of deduction types as a percent of sales can provide the basis for a flat allowance percent granted to the customer instead of the customer taking deductions.

12. A periodic review of the cost of processing and controlling deductions vs. the benefit achieved. The cost of deduction processing is the cost of the staff performing the function with an

▶ CASE HISTORY ◀

Two Cases of Deductions Adding to the Bottom Line

Case One

The distributor mentioned earlier in this section, which had no deductions processing capability and just wrote them off at 180 days old, implemented a formal deductions process. Deductions were routed to the department best positioned to resolve them (i.e., contract administration for pricing deductions, logistics for shipping deductions). Standard resolution times were enforced and performance metrics introduced. Invalid deductions were challenged, and, in many cases, the distributor discovered customers were deducting based on outdated price lists. Invalid deductions were charged back to customers and collected at an annual rate of $500,000, which was all increased profit. Past due receivables over 90 days old were reduced by 70%.

Case Two

The food products manufacturer mentioned earlier in this section redesigned its deductions processing, incorporating most of the Best Practices presented earlier. Open deductions decreased by 76%. The aging profile of open deductions improved substantially, and recovery of invalid deductions increased over 40%.

allocation of overhead for facility, IT, and sales and management time utilized. The benefit is the amount of invalid deductions recovered (collected, not merely charged back). In addition, there is a benefit for deterrence. Although this is difficult to quantify, it should be taken into consideration.

Key Points

The four important elements of deduction processing are:

1. Deduction processing is inherently a low-value-added activity. Essentially, it results in 95% of deductions being adjusted or written off, and only a few percent being collected from customers. Who wants to spend a lot of money on such an activity?

2. If deductions are not researched and checked for validity in some manner, losses from invalid deductions will be significant and increase over time.

3. Deductions must be dealt with. That is why it is vitally important to have a formal process leveraged with technology. The necessary "policing" can be performed at the lowest cost.

4. Deduction reduction is the best solution accomplished by improving internal order fulfillment and invoicing operations, and by confronting abusive customers.

LATE PAYMENT FEES AND PROMPT PAYMENT DISCOUNTS

Overview

Late payment fees and prompt payment discounts are incentives designed to encourage customers to pay according to terms. Prompt payment discounts offer a reward for paying "early," and late payment fees are a penalty for paying late. If implemented properly, they can have a substantial impact in improving receivables management results.

Late payment fees (also known as finance charges, interest charges, or service charges) are an assessment of the interest value of a customer enjoying the use of funds beyond the due date. Payment terms are widely considered an integral part of the price, so if a customer is taking a longer period to pay than agreed, the customer is receiving more value than the price being paid. In evaluating price discrimination under the Robinson-Patman Act, the courts have usually included payment terms in the pricing equation.

The interest rate used in the assessment varies, but it is an attempt by the seller to recoup the extra borrowing cost it incurs as a result of a late payment. In many states it is limited by usury laws. The most common rate we have seen is 12% per annum. In the early 1980s, when the prime rate was in the 18 to 21% range, many companies that had not assessed late payment fees initiated the practice. Rates were set at 18% or higher, often the highest rate allowed by law.

The major difficulty with late payment fees is customers' refusal to pay them. Many accounts payable departments are under standing orders from the chief financial officer to never pay late payment fees. Collecting them is difficult.

Prompt payment discounts can be an extremely powerful but expensive tool to expedite payments. To illustrate, consider the payment terms defined as "1% 10 days, net 30 days from date of invoice." These terms enable the customer to deduct 1% from the total invoice amount if it is paid within 10 days from invoice date. If the customer does not exercise this option, then the full amount of the invoice is due within 30 days of the invoice date. When interest rates are low, the 1% prompt payment discount is very attractive. Even if the customer has to borrow money to pay within 10 days, it is cost effective to do so. If a company is operating on a low gross margin, the extra 1% margin can be extremely valuable.

The major difficulty with prompt payment discounts is when customers pay well beyond the discount period due date yet still take the prompt payment discount. This is known as an unearned discount and is usually charged back to the customer. Many accounts payable departments follow a policy of taking all prompt payment discounts offered, regardless of when the invoice is paid. Collecting unearned discounts is difficult.

Prompt Payment Discount Works for Supplier and Customer

The customer, a distributor of medical products, operated on a very low (6%) gross margin. One-third of that gross margin derived from a prompt payment discount offered by its suppliers. The prompt payment discount was so important to the distributor's profitability, it always paid its invoices early enough to earn the discount. The customer routinely borrowed on a short-term line of credit to do so. The cost of borrowings was well below the benefit of the 2% prompt payment discount.

The supplier found that the prompt payment discount was very effective in securing prompt payments. However, it cost the supplier two percentage points off of its gross margin, which exceeds the cost of funding the receivables for the full payment term. The supplier was in a high-margin business and wanted to preempt receivables issues with its customers by offering an attractive prompt payment discount, so it was worth it to the supplier. *Both parties benefited from the prompt payment discount.*

Best Practices

Best Practice for both late payment fees and prompt payment discounts are similar. The five Best Practices include:

1. Commitment. The *absolutely essential* first requirement for the successful implementation of late payment fees and prompt payment discounts is a total company commitment to their enforcement. By total company commitment, we mean all functions within a company, especially sales, customer service, and general management as well as finance. The commitment must be shared at the most senior levels of the firm. This commitment is critical to presenting and maintaining a united front to the customer base. Inevitably, large and valuable customers will balk at paying late payment fees or unearned prompt payment discounts. If the resolve to enforce the terms does not exist, the

implementation of these tools will progressively deteriorate. *If a high level of commitment does not exist, it is best to avoid late payment fees and prompt payment discounts.* Without the necessary commitment, all that will result is the creation of a huge volume of late payment fees and unearned prompt payment discounts that will have to be adjusted or written off. This added workload, plus the defeat of the initiative, will reduce staff morale. In addition, the customers that do abide by the policy will be punished for their good behavior. If word gets out into the marketplace that some firms are flaunting the terms, a great deal of ill will can be generated among customers that are following the terms.

2. Automation of the creation of late payment fees and unearned prompt payment discounts. These are high-volume, low-value transactions that can consume a great deal of staff time unless completely automated. Other operations to automate are:

    a. The notification to customers of the assessment of a late payment fee or an unearned prompt payment discount. Since most of these notices are disregarded, an option is to just post them to the customer account so they will be included in the monthly statements of account sent to customers.

    b. The adjustment or write-off of the transactions. Inevitably, a large number of these transactions will be adjusted as a result of negotiation with customers.

3. The use of a grace period for the due dates. If a customer payment arrives a few days beyond the due date, do you really want to assess a late payment fee or deny a prompt payment discount? It will be very difficult to enforce a charge for a payment that is a few days late, and even if you secure payment, it will generate ill will with the customer. A grace period allows a payment to arrive a specified number of days beyond the due date and still be considered on time for the purposes of assessing a late payment fee or unearned prompt payment discount. Best Practice defines an optimal grace period at five to eight days. Of course, every attempt should be made to keep the existence of a grace period confidential. Otherwise, customers will build it into their payment cycle.

4. Utilization of a late payment fee and/or a prompt payment discount as a collection tool. This practice is extremely useful in proactive customer contact. It reinforces the customer service aspect of a proactive call. A suggested approach would be to point out invoices that are in danger of aging beyond eligibility for a prompt payment discount or that will incur a late payment fee. In essence, the call is to alert the customer to an opportunity to save money.

   Late payment fees and/or prompt payment discounts can also be used as bargaining chips. A limited amount of such charges can be conceded in return for a customer bringing the account current or taking another action. Collectors should be unilaterally empowered to concede a limited amount of such charges.

5. Booking late payment fees and unearned prompt payment discounts to a suspense account instead of directly to interest income or revenue. Unless you are collecting over 90% of such charges, booking them in the accounting ledger to an income account can cause significant revenue variations in some months.

► CASE HISTORY ◄

The selection of case histories for this section was easy. Of the over 100 companies with whom we have worked on receivables management, only 2 have successfully implemented late payment fees. All the rest have struggled with a huge volume of very small value transactions that are generated, posted to customer accounts, receive halfhearted collection efforts, age, clutter the receivables ledger, and are eventually written off, all the while sapping staff time from more productive activities.

Success Story One
A high-technology company was in dire financial straits and was seeking improvement in revenue and costs every way possible. This environment engendered the management resolve necessary to enforcing

(continues)

Case History (*continued*)

a late payment fee program. The program was launched, incorporating the Best Practices mentioned above, and supported by the highest levels of senior management. Enforcement was achieved even with large, valuable customers. After six months, the largest benefit was a 19% reduction in DSO, which enabled the firm to reduce its debt and interest expense with the newly generated cash. Income from late payment fees was significant (approximating several tenths of 1% of total revenue) during the first six months, but afterward decreased to less than 1/10 of 1 percent of revenue. As customers were educated to the resolve of the program, many of them changed their payment behavior, which produced the reduction in DSO.

Success Story Two
A refiner of precious metals supplied independent jewelry manufacturers. The majority of its customers were very small, undercapitalized companies, whose business was heavily skewed by seasonality. These customers had to manufacture their products through the summer, ship them to retailers in the fall, and receive payment in January. They needed financing, but most were unable to secure financing from banks. As part of their business strategy, the precious metal supplier extended payment terms to customers as a means of financing. The supplier assessed a financing fee and late payment fees, and collected 97% of them. The financing and late payment fees were an integral part of doing business and were well understood by customers and the supplier's sales force. Enforcement was strongly supported by senior management. The financing and late payment fees were a substantial contributor to revenue and profit.

Key Points

The two key points to remember about late payment fees and prompt payment discounts are:

1. Do not utilize these techniques unless senior management is fully committed and willing to stay the course through some trying times.

2. Automate the process.

► **CASE HISTORY** ◄

Prompt Payment Success Story

The case history for prompt payment discounts is similar to those of late payment fees. This case history illustrates a success, but at a high cost.

A manufacturer of auto parts for the aftermarket sold to a network of dealers. Many of the dealers were small, thinly capitalized businesses that presented a considerable risk of bad debt loss. Industry practice was to extend payment terms to 90 to 120 days. In an effort to meet competition but control credit risk, the manufacturer offered a series of attractive prompt payment discounts. With a net due date of 90 days from invoice date, the discounts were structured for 1% if payment was received 60 days from invoice date, 2% at 30 days, and 3% at 15 days from invoice date. The impact on receivables was impressive. On average, 95% of receivables were current, with little delinquency and bad debt. However, the cost of the discounts was huge, averaging approximately 2% of revenue, or tens of millions of dollars. The cost vs. benefit of these terms can be debated, but they clearly had a beneficial impact on receivables management results.

DISPUTE MANAGEMENT

Overview

In our experience, at least half of receivables past due more than 15 days are disputed. Successful dispute management is essential to successful receivables management. It is not possible to achieve excellent receivables management results without a robust capability to identify, resolve, and clear disputes.

For receivables management purposes, a dispute is any unmet customer requirement or expectation that results in short payment or nonpayment of an invoice. Deductions (short payments) are a subset of disputes, and there are many similarities between deduction and dispute management.

Disputes arise from:

- Customer dissatisfaction with the product or service delivered. We estimate that disputes of this type account for approximately one-third of all disputes.

- An inaccurate or inadequate invoice. We estimate that this cause accounts for approximately two-thirds of all disputes. Remember the importance attached to invoicing accuracy discussed earlier in this book.

The occurrence of disputes is unavoidable. Even if every order is fulfilled and billed perfectly, disputes will occur because:

- The customer mistakenly perceives an error has been made.

- The customer raises a dispute to delay paying the invoice.

Dispute reduction is a valuable activity, and we will address it later under Best Practices. The most common flaw we have seen in companies' receivables management capability is the ability to promptly identify, resolve, and clear those disputes that occur. Why does this inability afflict so many firms? The most common attitudes (and accompanying processes) are:

- "It's not my job. If the collectors want the past due invoice cleared, it's their job to research, resolve, and clear it."

- "Customer satisfaction is everybody's job. If a customer expresses dissatisfaction with something, everyone will stop what they're doing and fix it."

- "The customer is right, but we cannot afford to issue a credit and take the hit to revenue this month." We expect this reason will be given much less frequently as people learn the implications of Sarbanes-Oxley.

These comments all reflect the absence of a formal process to identify, research, resolve, and clear disputes, as well as measurement of the organization's performance in doing so.

The results of the lack of an informal or ad hoc process can be devastating. They include:

- Elevated delinquency.

- Excessive credits, allowances, and concessions that decrease revenue and profitability. The greater the elapsed time, the greater the probability that a credit will be granted, even if the customer is wrong. The deterioration of people's memories, the degradation of documentation, and the turnover of staff on both sides increase the tendency to concede.

- Unhappy customers. Customers may like your product or service, but may find conducting business with your firm very difficult. Waiting long periods of time for a credit memo is particularly vexing for customers. Inaccurate billing and poor administration of a customer's account may affect your supplier quality rating with your customers, which can ultimately lead to lower sales volume.

- Lower productivity from handling, reconstruction, and rehandling disputes over an elongated time frame.

Best Practices

Seven Best Practices for excellence in dispute management include:

1.   Establishment of a policy and formal process to manage disputes. The formal process should have defined work flows, procedures, roles and responsibilities, and ownership. Training should be conducted of all participants in the process and users of the reports, so the objective and operation of the process is understood. All participants must understand their role in the process and its importance.

    The seven-step process must include:

    a. Well-defined work flows from identification of a dispute through to clearing it from the receivables ledger. A common trap is to forget about a dispute when it is classified as resolved. Remember, the ultimate objective is to clear a dispute from the receivables through a payment, credit, or combination of both. The job is not finished until the dispute is entirely cleared.

b. Prompt identification of disputes, not just by collection staff, but by all customer-facing functions of the company, such as sales, customer service, and so on.

c. Routing of disputes to the person in the organization who generated the disputed element and is best positioned to resolve it. To illustrate this concept, consider a dispute where the customer claims to have been charged the wrong price. The pricing or contract administration function can usually determine in a minute or two if the invoiced price is correct. People in this position work with the pricing system every day and can navigate it very quickly. Conversely, a person outside this department may spend 5 to 20 minutes performing the same research. It is to the company's benefit to research the dispute most efficiently; therefore, the pricing/contract administration group should be assigned to this dispute. In addition, it is likely that this group is the root cause of the error. Routing pricing disputes to this group alerts group members to the error so they can correct it for future transactions of the same type, thereby reducing the number of disputes incurred in the future. This also teaches the staff members that if they cause an error leading to a dispute, they will have to deal with it.

d. Establishment of a standard time frame for researching and resolving a dispute. This time frame sets the expectation of how fast the customer satisfaction issue will be resolved. It is usually set at several days. It is the performance standard that individuals, departments, and the entire organization will be measured against in evaluating dispute resolution performance.

e. Tracking of all disputes from identification through to clearing. This ensures that no disputes "fall through the cracks" and linger unresolved. Nothing enrages a customer more than to have to report, describe, and document the dispute more than once to different people. This tracking requires a system tool, which will be discussed under the automation element. Assignment of a discrete transaction number to each dispute is a simple way to facilitate tracking.

f. Categorization of all disputes by type and root cause. This facilitates correction efforts and the measurement of progress in correcting and reducing them.

g. Measurement and reporting of dispute management performance at an individual, department, and total organization level. This brings accountability to the organization and produces a part of the answer to the question: How are we treating our customers?

Four key metrics include:

a. Cycle time from identification of a dispute to clearing from the receivables ledger

b. Throughput analysis (number and value of disputes identified in a period vs. number and value cleared)

c. Backlog of unresolved disputes in aging categories

d. Ultimate outcome of disputes via cash payment or credit memo

2. Automation of the process with technology. Dispute management usually involves a high volume of transactions. To efficiently route, categorize, track, and report on them requires the speed, capability, and database capability of a system tool. The leading ERP applications have varying capability to manage and process disputes. As mentioned in the deductions processing section, many commercially available applications automate the dispute management function. These applications, sometimes called "bolt-ons," are compatible with most ERP systems and enhance the dispute management functionality. Often the applications provide credit, collection, and/or deduction processing

► CASE HISTORY ◄

Dispute Categorization Offers Solutions

A publishing company initiated categorization of disputes by type. After a few weeks, it concluded that the leading cause of customer disputes was sales and use tax discrepancies. To correct the problem, the company installed a leading sales and use tax software tool, which greatly increased its accuracy in charging such taxes. After a few months, company metrics showed that sales tax disputes decreased dramatically.

The same company discovered that disputes concerning a certain type of display advertisement were the second most frequent dispute type. Customers were sending the ad text to the publisher, where the text was retyped into its publishing system. Inevitably, a large number of transcription errors were made. The solution implemented was to cut and paste customers' electronic submission into the publishing system. This dramatically decreased disputes of this type as errors were virtually eliminated and errors that did occur were the customers' fault.

capability as well as dispute management. These applications also provide the reporting and query functionality required.

3. The ability to attach images of documents, e-mails, approval forms, and other information to the dispute as it is routed through the process. This important feature of the leading dispute management automation enables a recipient to view pertinent information and documents that another person has already researched. This is a huge productivity improvement. In addition, the work flows of dispute types can be designed into the application to facilitate routing and processing.

4. Development of a culture that views disputes as an opportunity to improve customer satisfaction, not as an event that places blame on individuals within the organization. Dispute management is a customer service, not a finance or credit department task. A leading auto manufacturer discovered through customer

surveys that customers who experienced a problem and had it fixed promptly had a higher incidence of repeat purchases than customers who had never experienced a problem.

5. Support and reinforcement by senior management that dispute management is an interdepartmental function to improve customer satisfaction, not a collection process.

6. Initiation of a formal, continuous improvement program whose objective is to correct the root causes of the high-frequency disputes to ultimately reduce the number of disputes incurred.

7. Compilation and comparison of disputes by customer to identify:

   a. Customers who are receiving poor-quality service and who may be at risk of defecting to the competition

   b. Customers who may be utilizing disputes to slow their payment of invoices.

Key Points

The six key points include:

1. Disputes are the leading cause of receivables delinquency.

2. Excellence in receivables management is not possible without an effective and efficient dispute management process.

3. Dispute management requires a formal, robust process and an organizational commitment to customer satisfaction.

4. Technology to automate the process is essential.

5. A continuous improvement program to reduce the causes of high-frequency disputes will decrease the volume of future disputes and improve customer satisfaction, productivity, and receivables management results.

6. Measurement of performance is critical to improvement in dispute management.

► CASE HISTORY ◄

Two Dispute Management Success Stories

Success Story One
A high-technology provider lacked a formal dispute management process. Visibility of dispute resolution performance was poor. Receivables management results were disappointing, with a high level of past due invoices. Analysis of delinquent receivables revealed that once an invoice aged over 30 days past due, there was a high probability that it would remain open for several months longer. This finding is indicative of a poor dispute process. As a result, cash flow and staff productivity were significantly impacted.

The company implemented a formal dispute process incorporating most of the Best Practices listed above. Over 500 staff members in multiple departments were trained in the operation and culture of dispute management.

After six months of operation, these results were realized:

- The average cycle time from identification of a dispute to clearing was reduced from 238 days to 86 days.
- Total past due receivables were reduced by 24%. Receivables over 90 days past due were decreased by half.
- Customer satisfaction with administrative service increased by 30%.
- Staff productivity increased by 41%.

Success Story Two
A publishing firm was dealing with a large number of disputes with a combination of an ad hoc process and multiple manual lists of open disputes. Ownership of the process and accountability for results were unclear. Many disputes were not formally identified as individuals attempted to deal with them off line. Over two-thirds of open disputes were over 60 days old.

The company implemented a formal dispute process with many of the features included in Best Practices. After only four months of operation, 95% of open disputes were less than 14 days old. The level of open disputes was reduced by $7 million, enabling a reduction in the reserve for credits and allowances. Total delinquency and DSO were reduced by 22% and 16% respectively.

ACCOUNT MAINTENANCE

Overview

Account maintenance is the process of removing clutter from a customer's account. As mentioned, "clutter" describes all the open transactions on a customer's account except whole invoices. Clutter includes deductions (short-paid invoices), unapplied cash, credit memos, chargebacks, unearned discounts, late payment fees, and so on. All of these transactions sum into the total balance owed by a customer. Clutter can cause numerous problems including:

- Customer confusion or disagreement as to how much is owed and how much is due at any point in time. This confusion and/or disagreement makes it very difficult for a collector to collect receivables. At the very least, it reduces collectors' productivity as they will have to research, document, and explain to the customer the nature of these open items. Often the clutter serves as a diversion of a collector's efforts. A collector may call a customer to collect large, whole open invoices, but the customer may insist on discussing the clutter items first. Since many of the clutter items are of relatively small value, the result is the collector spending time resolving small-value items, while the large-dollar invoices receive inadequate attention.

- Customer dissatisfaction with the administrative quality of the supplier. When customers receive their monthly statement of account, and it contains many old clutter items, they may conclude that their account is not being serviced and maintained well. One of the key objectives of receivables management is to maintain customer accounts in good order to facilitate the unencumbered flow of business. It is a service provided to customers. This is why many companies call their receivables management departments customer financial services. A cluttered account is the antithesis of customer financial service.

- Difficulty during an internal or external audit for both the customer and the supplier. If the auditors want to confirm the balance owed by a customer and there is a lot of clutter on the account, the amount recorded by the customer as a payable will not agree with the amount on the monthly statement of account. This may trigger a time-consuming reconciliation at a very intense, busy time of year and will certainly annoy the customer.

- Higher cost in securitizing, collateralizing, factoring, selling, or other method of financing that pledges the receivables asset. If a large amount of clutter exists in the portfolio, a lender will disqualify it from the valuation of the asset. This can result in the lender/financier lending much less than the book valuation of the receivables asset, charging a higher risk-adjusted interest rate, or both. For example, instead of receiving financing equal to 90% of the book value of the receivables at the prime rate plus 100 basis points, the lender may only be willing to lend 80% of the value at 250 basis points above prime. Often the clutter that diminishes the realizable value of the receivables is referred to as dilution.

- Greater bad debt expense. The accumulation of clutter in the oldest-aging categories will cause those amounts to be reserved for, which incurs bad debt expense each month. If they are collectable, their collectability will decrease over time. The ultimate collection will be higher the earlier they are dealt with. If they are not collectable, that determination should be made as early as possible, and the item should be cleared from the receivables ledger. This will avoid overstating assets, profit, and revenue, which is critically important under Sarbanes-Oxley.

Best Practices

Exhibit 3.9 presents Best Practice in account maintenance, illustrating the receivables portfolio as a repository of inflows and outflows.

The receivables portfolio receives a constant input of new transactions:

- Invoices

> ▶ **CASE HISTORY** ◀

Sloppy Account Maintenance Proves Costly

A service company had a very large customer that accounted for over 10% of revenue. The service company's business involved thousands of low-value transactions per month with this large customer. Accurate pricing of invoices was a problem, resulting in hundreds of deductions and disputes incurred each month. Resolution and clearing of these deductions and disputes lagged well behind the rate of creation of these clutter items. Over a two-year period, 16,000 clutter transactions accumulated, most in the oldest-aging category. The transactions were:

- 14,000 deductions
- 1,200 unapplied payments
- 800 unapplied credit memos
- 250 chargebacks

Their net value was several million dollars, which was reserved for at a very high percentage. The result of the failure to maintain the account of this major customer was:

- An unhappy customer. The customer attended numerous meetings to resolve the problem, but it kept getting worse. The customer felt it was not being serviced and threatened to take its business elsewhere.
- A loss of several hundred thousand dollars of invalid deductions that would have been collected if they were charged back on a timely basis.
- A workload of almost one person-year of work to research and resolve the 16,000 clutter items.

Clearly, failure to maintain this customer account in a clean state had a serious impact.

- Payments
- Credit memos
- Chargebacks
- Late payment fees
- Unearned discounts

Exhibit 3.9 Receivables Holding Tank

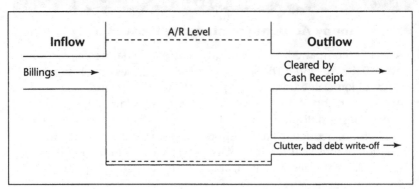

Ideally the credit transactions match and clear the debit transactions, leaving only whole open invoices. The perfect portfolio would contain only current, whole open invoices.

In order to approach the perfect, uncluttered state, the unmatched clutter transactions must be cleared continuously and on a timely basis. Unfortunately, there is no magic to this. It requires a process that is diligently executed every week. The eight key elements of this process are:

1. A policy that recognizes the low value and low collectability of most of the clutter. Too many companies cling to small, old amounts of doubtful value. In many cases, the cost of tracking them and attempting collection exceeds the expected payback. Best Practice policy mandates the write-off of most clutter debits at a defined age, often 180 days.

2. Automatic small-balance write-off in cash application. This eliminates many clutter items as soon as incurred for a minor financial impact.

3. Purging of small-value, aged credit balances, such as credit memos and unapplied payments. A list of purged transactions should be kept to provide an audit trail should a customer inquire about them in the future. Escheat laws should also be reviewed and obeyed when purging unapplied payments.

4. Empowerment of collection staff members to concede clutter transactions below a defined value as part of their negotiations and client service.

5. Automated execution of the purges.

6. Manual adjustments executed by lower-cost administrative or clerical staff, and not by collectors.

7. Automated matching and clearing of credit memos to invoices using the invoice number as the reference number.

8. Sound deduction, dispute, and reconciliation processes.

Key Points

The two key points to remember about account maintenance are:

1. Lack of good account maintenance can have substantial deleterious effects on receivables management. Many of the impacts are hidden and take time to accumulate. Account maintenance is often overlooked when dealing with boosting cash collections or dealing with large, problem customers. However, if neglected too long, it will impact receivables management results, customer service, and efficiency.

2. A disciplined approach with automatic clearing built into policy and process will solve the majority of clutter buildup in the portfolio.

PAYMENT PROCESSING

Overview

Payment processing, also known as cash application, is the process of applying customer payments, credit memos, and adjustments to open debit obligations (usually invoices) on a customer's account to match and clear them. Payment processing refers to payments in all its forms:

- Checks
- Electronic payments such as wire transfers and Automated Clearing House (ACH) payments
- Credit, debit, and procurement card payments
- Actual currency

The objectives of payment processing are to:

- Deposit funds received in the company bank account as quickly as possible. Usually this function is performed prior to applying payments for internal control and segregation of duties reasons. The passage of the "Check 21" banking law, which became effective October 28, 2004, will reduce "float" time and give companies faster use of the money received via paper check.

- Match the payments to open debits on the proper customer account accurately and quickly, and clear the transactions.

Perfect performance for payment processing would be to apply 100% of payments accurately and on the same business day they were received. This perfection is rarely if ever achieved for a variety of reasons, which will be discussed later.

When payment processing is performed well, it is usually unnoticed. It is when errors or backlogs emerge that the function receives attention. The two major problems encountered with payment processing are a backlog of unapplied payments and inaccurate application of payments. Of the two, misapplication of payments is the more damaging.

Backlog of Unapplied Payments

Customer payments that are unapplied more than a few days after receipt date can cause several problems:

- The first is wasted collection effort. If a customer has paid, but the payment has not been posted, a collection letter or collection call may be triggered. Collecting an invoice that has already been paid is pure, 100% waste.

- Customer annoyance. Collection activity on an invoice that has been paid wastes customer time as well as vendor time. It also serves to annoy the customer. It is poor customer financial service and degrades the customer's perception of the vendor as a quality operation.

- It adds to the clutter on a customer's account and in the total receivables portfolio. The deleterious effects of clutter were described in the preceding section.

The causes of a backlog of unapplied payments are usually:

- The customer's remittance advice (i.e., instructions on how to apply the payment) is missing or unclear. This is commonly known as unapplied cash, as it can be posted to the proper customer account, but not matched to an open obligation.

- The payment processing staff members are unable to identify which customer has sent the payment. Believe it or not, this happens much more frequently than you would expect. It can be caused by a change in the customer's name due to a merger or acquisition. It can be caused by the customer's legal name being different from the trade name under which it conducts business. Either cause can confuse cash appliers. You would think that companies would want to ensure that they receive credit on their account for money they send to suppliers, but "unidentified" cash is a common occurrence.

- The payment processing staff is not keeping up with the volume of incoming payments. This can be caused by understaffing or underperformance of the staff.

Misapplication or Inaccurate Posting of Payments

As in invoicing, while both speed and accuracy are important, *accuracy is much more important, because the results of misapplied payments are devastating.* Correction of unapplied cash may require contacting the customer and performing some research, but generally it is not too time consuming. However, correcting a misapplied payment can require an enormous amount of time. It will involve reversing the erroneous application and performing the correct application. Seems easy enough. However, if the misapplication occurred well in the past, it may require *every payment applied since the error to be reversed and reapplied.* For a high-volume customer, this can be a lot of work. If misapplications were

---

▶ CASE HISTORY ◀

Misapplication of Payments

An apparel manufacturer sold to over 10,000 customers, most of whom were small-volume accounts. Poor management of the payment processing function caused the manufacturer to apply all customer payments to the oldest open obligations, disregarding customer remittance advice. This misapplication continued for six months over a high volume of payments before senior management intervened.

The results were catastrophic. Thousands of payments were misapplied, affecting thousands of customer accounts. Each month when statements of account were sent to customers, there was a flood of incoming calls from customers disputing the status of their accounts. Most of the calls regarded invoices the customers had paid, but were shown as open and past due on the statement of account because of misapplication of the payments. Customers were annoyed and enraged, and demanded the statements be revised and reissued. Hundreds of customers ceased all payments until they received an accurate statement of account. The credit and customer service departments were paralyzed by the volume of calls and the task of correcting customer accounts. No outbound collection calls were made for several months.

Cash flow dropped substantially. Overhead costs increased dramatically because of the temporary labor hired to correct the inaccurate payment posting. A workload of several person-years of work confronted the company. Concessions increased to appease angry customers. The misapplication of payments was threatening the very profitability of the company.

made to numerous customer accounts, then the rework increases multiplicatively. This type of corrective effort can consume dozens of hours of work for a single customer.

In addition to rework, the misapplication will cause customer dissatisfaction. In some cases, it may cause customers to withhold all future payments until their accounts are reconciled and cleaned up. When customers adopt this posture, it:

- Decreases cash flow

- Imposes an urgent rework requirement

If many customers adopt the same stance simultaneously, the impact on cash flow can be serious. In addition, the rework burden mushrooms, and all the rework must be performed quickly to induce customers to resume payments. This could be considered a crisis.

The cause of misapplication is usually human error and lack of commitment to get it right. If a customer's application instructions are unclear, always contact the customer and secure clarification. Payments should never be applied unilaterally; they should always be applied consistently with the customer's directions. It is that simple. One company with which we have worked has a policy of immediate termination of any payment processor who applies a payment without written instruction from the customer. Undoubtedly, the company learned from experience.

Best Practices

Best Practices for payment processing rely on a strong commitment to accuracy and "doing it right," balanced against the need to apply payments promptly. The staff members who process payments should have diligence, attention to detail, and a thorough knowledge of customer accounting. The other seven major elements of Best Practices in payment processing are:

1. Auto-cash technology. This technology and how to optimize it

could be the subject of a book all by itself. At a summary level, it enables the payment processing/accounts receivable application to automatically:

a. Identify the customer account to which the payment should be posted. This is accomplished by the system matching the Magnetic Image Character Recognition (MICR) number on the check or the customer number specified in the electronic remittance data to the MICR number or customer number in the customer master file, then to the proper customer account in the receivables ledger.

b. Identify the open obligation on the customer account to which the payments apply, then match and clear the two transactions.

Often the payment data required is prepared by the lockbox processor while depositing the funds into your account. The data are sent by the bank and read by the auto-cash function.

The auto-cash function locates open obligations to apply payments based on predetermined decision rules programmed in the system. These rules (called algorithms) can be simple or quite complex. For example, the rule may require an exact match of the transaction (invoice) number and the amount for an automatic match. If both conditions are not present, the auto-match will not be executed, and it will have to investigated manually. Alternatively, the rule may be set to accept either of the two conditions to execute an automatic match and clearing. The less stringent the rules, the higher the percentage of payments that will be automatically matched. This percentage is also known as the auto-cash hit rate. The degree of stringency is a decision each company has to make based on the level of control desired, the number of customers, transactions, and so on. Remember, the higher the percentage of payments automatically matched, the less manual work is required. This increases speed and reduces cost.

The value of auto-cash cannot be overstated. Without it, 100% of payments have to be manually applied. Even with a poor hit rate of 50% (70 to 80% is common), the manual work is cut in half. What other administrative functions do you know of where 50 to 80% or more of the manual work can be eliminated?

c. Most ERP systems have auto-cash functionality in the accounts receivable modules. Many commercially available credit and collection automation applications have it as well. Thousands of companies use it, and activating it is not difficult. Activation may require changes in the internal process and in the way your lockbox processor presents data. However, the benefits are well worth the effort and cost. Other tips for auto-cash include: Allow the auto-cash application to match and clear individual payments contained within a remittance. A company with which we have worked has its algorithms structured so that the entire check must be automatically applied or the payment will be rejected, thereby requiring manual application of the entire payment. An example of this structure is in applying a customer check that paid 88 invoices. All but one payment matched an open invoice exactly, yet the entire payment was rejected for one exception. The result: Instead of one invoice being manually matched and cleared, all 88 were.

d. Allow the auto-cash application to apply short payments and create a separate deduction item. This is important if you incur many deductions from your customers. Structure the algorithm so that if the customer and invoice number matches that on the remittance advice, but the amount is less than the invoice, match and clear the invoice and payment, and post a deduction to the customer account. This can raise the hit rate substantially.

e. Build an automatic write-off of small balances into the algorithms. Clear the transaction immediately and automatically.

f. Over time, analyze the rejects and their root causes. If it is the behavior of certain customers, contact them and try to get them to remit in a manner that will raise the hit rate. Some of the rejects can be accepted with refinements to the algorithms. For example, linking parent and child relationships may enable the function to identify the customer making the payment. For example, if GE is paying invoices posted to your account for Amersham (a recent acquisition of GE), the parent-child linkage will enable automatic matching of the GE payment with the Amersham invoice. Sophisticated users have even built-in mathematical testing designed to identify transposition errors in invoice numbers. All of these refinements raise the hit rate and reduce workload.

2. Adopt a strict policy of complying with customer payment instructions at all times. If there is any doubt as to which open items a customer wishes to pay, contact the customer and secure its guidance. A confirming e-mail from the customer is desirable. Many payment processors with whom we have worked are reluctant to contact the customer directly. Some route the request for clarification through the collection staff. This involves an extra step but has the advantage of precipitating another contact between the collector and the customer. Whichever method is chosen, *contact the customer. Do not guess. This guarantees accuracy.*

3. Write-off small balance discrepancies automatically if possible, manually if necessary. Payment processing is the perfect stage to clear a transaction that will cost more money than it is worth to investigate and attempt to recover. The higher the write-off threshold, the more transactions will be quickly cleared, and the more time that will be saved.

4. Implement imaging of customer payments and remittance advices. This is the fastest way to retrieve this information when needed. Lockbox processors will usually offer this service for a fee. However it is arranged, it will enhance productivity. Images can be attached to e-mails, which accelerates transfer of information to customers and others within the company. This accelerates resolution of payment application discrepancies.

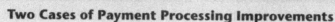

▶ CASE HISTORY ◀

Two Cases of Payment Processing Improvements

Case One

The apparel manufacturer mentioned earlier in this section implemented two major initiatives to recover from its problems. One was a reconciliation and recovery program designed to clean up the seriously cluttered portfolio. The other initiative was to redesign its payment processing, incorporating many of the Best Practices outlined in this section. The revamped payment processing maintained and advanced the progress made during the reconciliation and recovery program and prevented it from recurring. The results after one full year were impressive:

Open Item Type	Beginning	One Year Later
Credit memo	4756	1306
Unapplied cash	2351	658
Debit memos	6541	533

Case Two

A surgical products manufacturer initiated a two-part effort to improve its payment processing. The first was an accelerated program to research and correctly apply unapplied cash. The second was to improve the hit rate of its newly activated auto-cash function. Both initiatives utilized many of the Best Practices described in this section. After only six months, these results were achieved:

- Unapplied cash was reduced from $1.6 million to under $500,000.
- The auto-cash hit rate increased from 71 to 90%, largely as a result of the parent-child linkage explained above.

5. Continuously contact customers that do not send their remittance to the proper lockbox, and request them to change their remit address. Handling of misdirected payments usually involves manual effort. It slows cash flow and increases workload and cost. For many customers, a form letter requesting they send their payments to the proper address is not sufficient. A call is often required. The benefit is worth the effort.

6. Institute a continuous effort to research and apply "unapplied" and "unidentified" cash. It may make sense to have one or two staff members dedicate some time to specialize in this task. Specialization usually results in increased proficiency.

7. Establish targets and regular reporting of progress for these three payment processing metrics:

   a. Volume and value of incoming payments and payments completely applied

   b. Volume, value, and age of "unapplied" and "unidentified" cash

   c. Auto-cash hit rate

Key Points

The three key points about payment processing are:

1. Accuracy is paramount. Solicit and obey customer instructions on which open item payments apply.

2. Use auto-cash.

3. Measure throughput and backlog.

NOTE

1. Imany, Inc., seminar, "DSO Reduction: The Facts and Fallacies."

CHAPTER 4

Technology

OVERVIEW

This chapter gives an overview of technology in receivables management and the basic functionality required. It is not intended to be a technical treatise, but rather a general management perspective.

The proper use of technology is essential to achieving the effectiveness and the cost efficiency required of receivables management. However, it can be the object of overkill and the recipient of the blame for underperformance of the receivables management team. Receivables management success is more dependent on a sound process, staff skills and motivation, disciplined work habits, strong supervision, metrics, and incentives than on state-of-the-art technology. Technology drives cost efficiency and effectiveness, but is ineffective without the previously mentioned attributes. We have worked with effective credit and collection departments whose systems just reported invoice number, date, and amount in aging categories and allowed payment posting. While their efficiency suffered, they achieved strong aging and days sales outstanding (DSO) results. Beware the credit manager who blames all shortcomings on the technology or believes the solution is solely improved technology.

There are three major deficiencies with receivables management technology that can seriously affect receivables management. They are:

1. Lack of data integrity. If invoices, payments, and other transactions are not posting and deleting properly, or if balances change

131

in the absence of a legitimate transaction, this is a serious problem. It paralyzes the collection effort, which depends on knowing how much a customer owes and for which transactions. It can render collection letters and statements of account useless.

2. Inaccurate aging. This is fairly common. Many companies set their aging mechanism (or are restricted by their receivables application) for 30-day categories aged from invoice date. This is fine if 100% of invoices have payment terms of net 30 days. Unfortunately, the aging status (current or past due) of invoices with different payment terms will not be accurate. For example, an invoice with net 45-day payment terms will be displayed as 14 days past due when it is 44 days beyond invoice date. It is really current, not past due. Inaccurate aging forces a collector to examine each invoice to determine its aging status. This is time consuming and decreases productivity. Inevitably, collectors will call on an invoice they believe is past due. Customers will rebuke them. Not only is this wasted time, but it will reduce the morale and confidence of collectors and eventually make them gun-shy about making collection calls. Customers will gain the upper hand and doubt whatever they are told in the future. Inaccurate aging can also render collection letters and statements of account useless. Proper aging is from due date, not invoice date, and is very important to receivables management success.

3. Slow navigation among system screens and/or slow system response time. Typically, receivables staff members must consult multiple screens to gather required information and to perform operations. If it takes 10 seconds or more between screens, this will substantially impact productivity.

RECEIVABLES APPLICATIONS

Receivables applications are available in two major forms. One form is the module included in the enterprise resource planning (ERP) application that runs the entire company. Examples of well-known ERP software providers are Oracle, SAP, J.D. Edwards, and PeopleSoft (recent acquisitions of J.D. Edwards and PeopleSoft by Oracle notwithstanding). The advantage of the ERP modules is that they are fully integrated and compatible with the sales, billing, general ledger, and other functional modules serving the company. This is a huge advantage in efficiency, speed, and maintenance cost efficiency.

ERP receivables modules and their functionality have improved over the years. While they may not have the functionality, ease of use, and speed of specialized, commercially available credit and collections packages, they can provide most of the required functionality if configured properly. We have worked with a number of firms that complain about the limited functionality of their ERP receivables management modules, but that are not using it completely or properly.

The other major form is the commercially available, specialized credit and collection applications. Examples of providers of these packages are Get Paid, Emagia, E-credit, I-many, and 9ci, Inc. These packages, also known as bolt-ons, replace and/or supplement the ERP system's receivables management module with their own. These applications generally have more sophisticated functionality and improve receivables management effectiveness and efficiency. The providers of these applications claim that they are compatible with all major ERP systems and will provide consulting assistance in activating the application. The decision to utilize one of these packages depends on the cost versus benefits projected and will vary by individual company. Inclusion of the information technology (IT) department is essential to such a decision, as the compatibility and maintenance support issues must be evaluated by IT. Many users of such applications enthusiastically endorse them and attribute significant improvement in receivables management results to their use. Ultimately, the decision to use such an application comes down to the cost versus benefit analysis.

David A. Schmidt, principal of A2 Resources and a leading expert on receivables management automation, is a strong proponent of automation tools. He says:

> Receivables management is being transformed by automation. Credit and collection software provides work flow, data management, and analysis tools that have been lacking in even the best ERP systems. By

enabling access to all the information associated with the quote-to-cash process and then providing the tools to readily act upon that data, all from a single user interface, companies that have implemented receivables management software have realized dramatic improvements in performance as measured by reduced DSO and delinquencies. Greater efficiency, however, is only a part of the equation. The data gathered as a result of credit and collection activities provide a wealth of customer and process intelligence that can be used to increase customer profitability, invoice accuracy, and ultimately customer satisfaction. Used properly, receivables management automation is becoming the missing link between back office operations and front line customer relationship management.

BEST PRACTICES

Best Practices in receivables management technology utilization starts with the realization that technology is an important part, but only a part, of excellence in receivables management. Process, staff skills and motivation, senior management support, billing quality, supervision, metrics, and incentives are also important elements.

▶ CASE HISTORY ◀

Consequences of Not Aging Invoices Properly

A distributor operated a receivables application that did not age open invoices properly. It aged all invoices in 30-day categories from invoice date. Unfortunately, it sold customers on multiple terms, ranging from net 30 days all the way to net 120 days. Aging of the receivables asset was inaccurate, with past due receivables being significantly overstated. Prior to calling a customer, collectors had to analyze and reformat the open invoices to get a true picture of the past due amounts. This was time consuming and seriously reduced productivity. Outbound collection calls were well below the required volume, and collection letters and statements were not used. Cash flow suffered, and true delinquency was at elevated levels. Collector morale suffered.

The functionality of receivables management technology tools should include at least the six capabilities listed below. Customized capabilities to serve the unique needs of an individual business are critically important, but must be determined on an individual organization basis. The following six capabilities would be useful to most companies. The detailed technology capabilities required for each operation are included in each functional section in this book.

1. General capabilities

    a. Security, restricted access, and virus protection.

    b. Complete interface capabilities with general ledger, order entry, and billing.

    c. Ease of navigation among screens. This is best accomplished by linking screens through predetermined work flows or routines, so that information required is automatically presented to the user. For example, when reviewing a customer account in preparation for a collection call, a work flow will retrieve the customer master file or just the customer contact name, phone number, and e-mail address. Whether this is accomplished automatically or manually, it must be completed within several seconds.

    d. Electronic commerce capability including Electronic Data Interchange (EDI). This includes the ability to send, receive, and process orders, invoices, and payments with supporting information (e.g., remittance advice from the lockbox processor), the capability to direct debit a customer's bank account, execute any Automated Clearing House (ACH) or EFT transaction, and process credit, debit, and procurement card transactions.

    e. Imaging of documents available throughout the company and to customers via the World Wide Web. This capability serves most of the functions and operations within receivables management.

2. Credit control capabilities

a. Automated credit scoring of customers with ability to link directly into commercial credit reporting and/or credit scoring vendors.

b. Automatic order hold capability triggered by *either* an over-credit-limit or delinquency condition, or a bounced check, with the ability to exempt customers from automatic credit hold.

c. Robust customer master file capabilities, including credit limit (open, cash in advance, letter of credit, etc.) with expiration date, risk rating, parent-child linkage to other accounts, payment history and trend, complete customer contact, and ship-to and bill-to information.

3. Collection capabilities

a. Accurate aging of invoices by due date.

b. Truly automated collection letters with message and suppression capability and the ability to exclude disputed items.

c. Truly automated statements of account with message capability, plus the ability to generate and send one on demand.

d. Automated, accurate generation of unearned discounts and late payment fees, with allowance for a grace period, and generation of notices to customers.

e. Automated prioritization of accounts for collection action.

f. Automated customer contact, including auto-dialing, e-mail, fax, preformatted letters on demand.

g. Automated diary follow-up reminder.

h. Automated "look ahead" capability to view which invoices will fall due at a specified future date.

i. Notes capability at both the transaction and account level.

4. Dispute and deduction processing capabilities

a. Capacity to categorize with reason code and type.

    b. Assignment of unique, discrete transaction number.

    c. Routing to predetermined department based on reason code or type according to prescribed work flow.

    d. Ability to prioritize disputes based on preestablished criteria.

    e. Tracking of status through deletion from the receivables ledger.

    f. Capacity for multiple users to identify and process the disputes and deductions.

    g. Dunning capability for open disputes beyond the allowed resolution date.

    h. Robust reporting capabilities to report on disputes and deductions by type, resolver, status, age, and ultimate outcome.

5. Payment processing capabilities

    a. Auto-cash with the ability to modify algorithms as desired.

    b. Automatic small-balance write-offs.

    c. Automatic matching and clearing of credit memos and adjustments to open invoices and debits using the unique transaction number as a reference.

    d. Ability to assign reason codes to credit memos, adjustments, and write-offs.

    e. Easy navigation of the closed item ("paid history") files.

    f. Easy reversal of applied payments.

    g. Deduction processing capabilities.

6. Query and reporting capabilities

    a. Ability to easily generate a suite of standard reports to include aging, days sales outstanding (DSO), weighted average payment days (WAPD), and cash collected versus target.

    b. Excellent query capability to generate custom, one-time reports.

c. Ability to generate reports by collector, customer type or region, and so on. Query capability is extremely important for identifying opportunities to continually improve receivables management results. It provides the ability to analyze results and determine trends to diagnose emerging problems.

COST VERSUS BENEFIT

The cost versus benefit analysis is the key determinant in deciding the amount and cost of technology to utilize. Benefits derive from productivity (fewer full-time equivalents engaged in receivables management; this includes individuals deployed within the credit department and those external to the direct receivables management functions who devote a portion of their time to the task). Additional benefits derive from:

- Reduced bad debt expense
- Lower concessions of invalid deductions
- The funding savings from lower receivables
- The hard-to-quantify improvement in customer service

Costs are the direct costs of acquiring the technology, the start-up costs of activation, and the ongoing support and maintenance costs.

KEY POINTS

Three key points to remember include:

1. Technology is indispensable to achieving excellent receivables management results.
2. Technology alone cannot drive success in managing receivables.
3. Even a modest deployment of technology can bring substantial improvement in results and efficiency, so analyze the cost versus benefit, and do not be discouraged if the benefit does not justify a state-of-the-art system.

CHAPTER 5

Organizational Structure

OVERVIEW

The "right" organizational structure is one that will:

- Deploy the proper skills to each of the functions within receivables management to maximize effectiveness
- Staff the positions with the appropriate level of knowledge and experience to be cost efficient

The organizational structure defines how work is allocated among members of the organization, as well as the authority and reporting relationships. Economists refer to this allocation as "division of labor."

The resources and skills required are derived from the portfolio strategy. Each segment of the portfolio has a specific management approach, which defines the skill sets required. The amount of resource required is derived from the volumes handled.

In addition to allocating work among staff and defining the skill sets required, there are three major dimensions of organizational structure that must be addressed. They are:

1. Specialized versus enriched job content. Specialized job content means concentrating on a few tasks, which yields proficiency and efficiency. The disadvantage is that employees can become bored with a narrow range of tasks. Enriched job content means

139

a broad range of tasks. This promotes employee interest, development, and cross-training. The disadvantage is lower proficiency and productivity.

2. Utilization of a mix of part-time and full-time staff or only full-time staff. The advantage of part-time staff is:

    •   Part-time work instead of full-time work in repetitive processing tasks can reduce boredom.

    •   Part-time workers can often increase their work hours, which builds flexibility into department capacity.

    •   Part-time workers are often more cost efficient.

3. The number and span of control of supervisors and management. Companies with which we have worked often underestimate the level of supervision required to achieve peak effectiveness and efficiency. Other firms are top heavy as a result of a desire to reward good performers through a promotion to a supervisory or management position that is not really needed.

▶ CASE HISTORY ◀

Getting the Right People

A service company sold to thousands of customers, many of which were of small or medium size. Management of the receivables portfolio required a high volume of outbound collection calls to adequately penetrate the portfolio. A number of the collectors were uncomfortable with collection calling. As a result, whenever a dispute was encountered or a customer questioned their statement of account, these collectors performed hours of research and reconciliation to clean up the account and provide explanations to the customers. Therefore, their volume of outbound collection calls was inadequate. The company matched the wrong skill set (and desire) with the position and suffered inadequate cash collections as a result.

BEST PRACTICES

Best Practices in organizational design dictate that the structure must be tailored to each individual company, its sales and transaction volumes, its profitability, the number and risk profile of its customers, and its strategy and culture. No template can define the structure by filling in the blanks. However, the next eight Best Practices will help you design an effective and efficient organization.

1. Design the organization independently of the skill sets of the employees currently in the department. In other words, design it as if you were starting an entirely new organization with no employees yet hired. Naturally, the reality of business will induce you to populate the organization with existing staff, but the mismatches of skills and position requirements will at least be apparent. Actions such as training or staff replacement to correct the mismatches can then be planned and implemented.

2. Create specialized positions wherever possible, subject to the size limitations of the department. As mentioned, specialization promotes proficiency, productivity, and cost efficiency. In addition, the skill sets to perform the various functions within receivables management are quite different. The skills (and willingness) required to make collection calls are very different from those required to process payments and credit memos and reconcile customer statements. If all of these tasks are bundled into one enriched job, it is likely that one or more of the tasks will not be performed well. To make matters worse, some low-skilled tasks will be performed by high-skilled, high-cost staff. The different tasks and required skill sets (cryptically described) can be classified as shown in the table on the following page. Of course, adequate cross-training and backup capacity must be planned for specialized jobs.

3. Utilize part-time employees for some of the support positions. This is more cost efficient, and the part timers will be "fresher" in their work and provide backup and extra capacity when needed.

Task	Required Skills	Cost
Credit assessment	Financial evaluation	High
Collection: small accounts	High-volume customer contact	Medium
Collection: national accounts and government	Customer contact and account maintenance	High
Payment processing	Clerical accuracy	Low
Reconciliation	Clerical accuracy	Low
Dispute and deductions	Research, collaboration	Medium
Administrative support	Attention to detail	Low

4. Implement a program of periodic training to improve skill sets and provide cross-training in critical tasks. Training can be in the form of classroom, Web-cast, or side-by-side training, pairing an experienced teacher with a trainee. Of the three, side-by-side training is the most effective.

5. Create adequate supervision, but ensure the supervisory positions are not burdened with too much processing work. Receivables management requires a disciplined work effort performing the right actions, with consistent quality, in adequate volumes every day. Targets for key activities and results, and measurement of progress in achieving those targets, is a crucial management tool. Supervisors must monitor the work performed, reallocate peak workloads, and handle exceptions and escalations. If they are bogged down with busywork and cannot spend the majority of their time with the staff they supervise, results will not be optimized.

A good scheme for supervision is to have one supervisor for credit and collections staff and one for support functions. Support functions are the processing functions that do not involve frequent customer contact. Support functions include payment processing, dispute and deduction resolution, account reconciliation, and other administrative support. The scale of operations may not be sufficient to justify two supervisors. Conversely, if the span of control exceeds 10 to 12 staff members to one supervisor, additional supervisors may be needed.

6. Determine the level of resource needed based on transaction and customer volumes, service-level agreements (e.g., to process a credit application within 48 hours), and the company's overall strategy and financial targets. To determine the quantity of collectors, the model in Exhibit 5.1 is helpful.

   In the model shown in Exhibit 5.1, many of the variables can be modified to fit an individual company's circumstances. For example, the classification of the customers among "Poor," "Average," and "Good" can be used. Similarly, the call intensity levels, average call duration, and available hours can all be modified to more closely suit an individual company's environment. This model will yield a logical basis for determining the number of collectors needed.

   For support functions, determining the number of staff required is simple. Just take the normal run rate of incoming transactions in a day for a function (not a seasonal peak), and divide it by the number of transactions a competent staff member can process working seven hours in a day. This will yield the number of staff members required. Naturally, the calculated number can be adjusted by judgment.

7. Do not staff for peak volumes. Rely on part-time or temporary help and/or staff overtime to meet peak demands.

8. Try to avoid performing all of the research and resolution of disputes and deductions within the credit or receivables department. Disputes and deductions originate in many departments. The ability to resolve and prevent them in the future also resides within those departments.

The examples in Exhibits 5.2 and 5.3 are organizational structures designed utilizing most of the Best Practices described above. These structures can give a sense of the fundamentals of a good organization structure.

Exhibit 5.1 Collection Call Intensity Model

Account Segmentation	Percent Distribution	Number of Accounts	Contact Call Intensity Levels			Call Contact Volume		
			High	Medium	Low	Option 1	Option 2	Option 3
Major customers (79% of A/R $ and 24% of all accounts)								
Poor payers			4.0	3.0	2.0	0	0	0
Average payers	100	598	4.0	3.0	2.0	2392	1794	1196
Good payers			1.0	0.5	0.3	0	0	0
A segment	1005	598				2392	1794	1196
Midrange customers (15% of A/R $ and 24% of all accounts)								
Poor payers			2.0	1.0	0.8	0	0	0
Average payers	100	609	2.0	1.0	0.5	1218	609	305
Good payers			0.5	0.3	0.0	0	0	0
B segment	100	609				1218	609	305
Low-end accounts (6% of A/R $ and 52% of all accounts)								
Poor payers			1.0	0.8	0.5	0	0	0
Average payers	100	1311	0.5	0.3	0.3	656	437	328
Good payers			0.3	0.0	0.0	0	0	0
						656	437	328

			Contact Call Intensity Levels			Call Contact Volume		
Account Segmentation	*Percent Distribution*	*Number of Accounts*	*High*	*Medium*	*Low*	*Option 1*	*Option 2*	*Option 3*
All accounts		2518						
Total monthly call contact (outbound and inbound)						4266	2840	1829
Average working days in month				20				
Projected daily call volumes						213	142	91
Staffing of A/R collectors based on these assumptions:						*Option 1*	*Option 2*	*Option 3*

	Average Duration/Minutes	*Hours Available*	*Daily Capacity*	*Option 1*	*Option 2*	*Option 3*
A accounts	15	5.0	20	6.0	4.5	3.0
B accounts	10	6.0	36	1.7	0.9	0.4
C accounts	5	6.0	72	0.5	0.3	0.2
Total staffing under three intensity options				**8.2**	**5.7**	**3.6**
				8	**6**	**4**

Notes: Outbound call duration includes preparation and documentation time allowance.
Hours available provides allowance for account reconciliation and other administrative effort.

Exhibit 5.2 Sample Organization Chart

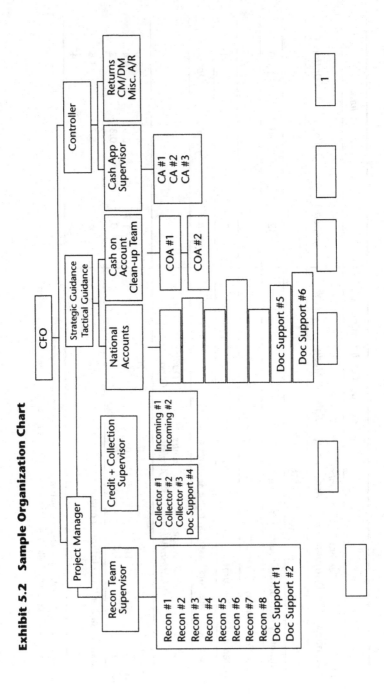

Exhibit 5.3 Credit and Collection Organization Chart

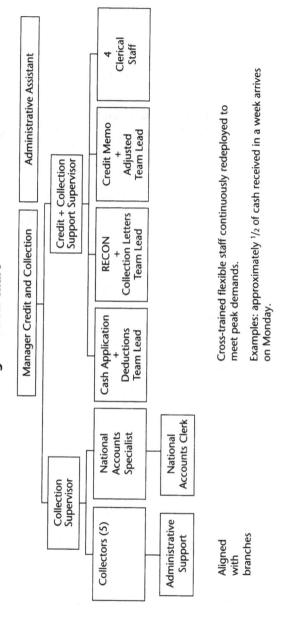

KEY POINTS

The organization structure has four key points:

1. The foundation of the organization structure is the portfolio strategy.

2. Receivables management tasks can be classified into two types: customer contact and processing support. These categories require very different skill sets performed by staff of very different cost levels.

3. Specialization drives effectiveness and cost efficiency.

4. Active supervision of daily work is a critical success factor.

CHAPTER 6

Metrics, Reporting, and Incentives

OVERVIEW

Receivables management is one of the most measurable business functions. The amount of cash collected, amount of receivables written off, amount within defined aging categories, and many other receivables dimensions are all finite numbers easily measured by accounting systems. This is fortunate, because conventional business wisdom states that you cannot manage that which you cannot measure.

This chapter addresses summary-level metrics for managing the receivables asset. Specialized metrics designed for industry-specific factors are not discussed here. Similarly, detailed metrics for individual functions performed in the management of the receivables asset are discussed in the sections dealing with that function (e.g., see the discussion on credit holds in Chapter 2).

Metrics and reporting are absolutely essential to successful management of the receivables asset. However, too much measurement and reporting, or overkill, will hurt results. Ideally, reporting of monthly results should consume no more than four hours of work per month. Analysis of the reports and taking action as a result of the reports should be the main focus. Everyone wants improved results; however, time spent reporting decreases the time spent improving results. Bear in mind that the objective is to improve results.

"REPORTING-DRIVEN DOWNWARD SPIRAL"

We have frequently observed a phenomenon we call the "reporting-driven downward spiral." This phenomenon starts when receivables results are below expectations. Senior management gets involved and begins requesting special reports and analyses. Usually the burden of producing these reports and analyses falls on the manager and staff of the receivables management function. A great deal of time is spent producing the special reports. Less time is available to actually drive improvement. As a consequence, the next month's results deteriorate, and there are even more requests for special analyses, meetings, and so on. All of these activities divert time from implementing actions to drive improvement, so results are disappointing again the following month. The continuing deterioration of results is the downward spiral.

The overriding principle in receivables metrics and reporting is to keep it simple and avoid consuming a great deal of time in their preparation. There are three basic types of receivables reports:

1. Measurements of results.

2. Monitoring of key activities that produce results.

3. Analyses of trends, root causes, and/or pockets of opportunities for improvement. These should be one-time analyses and reports, not recurring ones.

Metrics are most effective when compared to a target. Targets can be derived from historical performance, operating or financial budgets, or benchmarking against similar companies or those judged to be best in class.

Benchmarking is useful to obtain a general idea of the performance achieved by other organizations. It yields an order of magnitude of the difference between the selected companies' performance. However, the conditions under which that performance was achieved could be vastly different from the conditions under which your company operates (even if the company is in the same industry). In such cases, the comparison is not useful. This is especially true in receivables management where so many factors affect results. When benchmarking against another company's receivables management results, six influences can cause a huge difference in results achieved and can render the benchmark comparisons virtually useless:

1. *Billing quality.* If 15% of your invoices have errors and only 2% of the benchmarked company's invoices have errors, the receivables results can be very different, even if other factors are equivalent.

2. *Systems capability.* If one company's receivables management functions are highly automated and another's are manual, their results are not very comparable.

3. *Payment terms offered.* If one company offers net 30-day terms and another net 60, their respective days sales outstanding (DSO) will not be comparable. Exhibit 6.1 illustrates this effect.

4. *Strategy and management priorities.* If one company's strategy is to maximize revenue and tolerate the increased risk, its results will be very different from a company that is fiscally conservative and focuses on cash flow.

5. *The degree of export or overseas sales.* Payment practices for exports or overseas sales can be very different and can significantly impact results.

6. *The level of resources devoted to managing the receivables asset.* If one $500 million (annual sales) company uses 16 staff members to manage its receivables, and another $500 million company in the same industry uses only 5 staff members, their respective receivables management results will not be comparable.

In Exhibit 6.1, the company with the far left bar graph had a DSO of 51 and benchmarked itself against four other companies in its industry. Two companies had DSOs that were 8 to 12% higher, and the other two had DSOs 12% lower. The company performing the benchmarking concluded that there was modest improvement available. Unbeknownst to

Exhibit 6.1 Misleading DSO Benchmarking

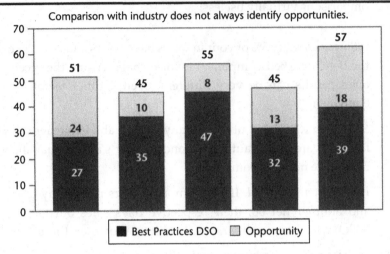

that company, it had the greatest opportunity for improvement among the five companies. Its best possible DSO of 27 days (a significant portion of its business was sold on net 15-day terms) was substantially lower than any of the companies in the benchmark study. Its gap between best possible and actual DSO was the highest (24 days, or 47%). However, since the company did not have insight into the other firms' payment terms, it mistakenly concluded that it was in line with the industry.

As stated earlier, the use of appropriate metrics is essential to receivables management success. Conversely, the use of the wrong metrics can hinder success, as these case histories illustrate.

BEST PRACTICES

The two Best Practices for reporting receivables management results include:

> ► **CASE HISTORY** ◄

Two Cases of Focusing on the Wrong Metrics

A service provider selected as its key receivables management metric the percent of receivables that were over 60 days past due. Naturally, the receivables management staff members focused their collection efforts on amounts over 60 days past due, which they drove to a relatively low level. Unfortunately, receivables over 60 days past due comprised only 10% of total receivables, which meant the other 90% of the asset was neglected. Receivables that were between 10 and 60 days past due received little attention and, as a result, were higher than they should have been. Correspondingly, DSO was much higher than it should have been. The company was overlooking a significant cash flow opportunity because of the performance metric it selected.

A beverage producer defined and measured its past due receivables as any amount greater than 30 days past due, in effect giving its customers a 30-day grace period. This definition led to a misstatement of past due receivables, a slight underaccrual of bad debt expense, and disguised a significant cash flow opportunity. Its definition of its key metric built in a substantial degree of ineffectiveness.

1. Report monthly and minimize the number of metrics routinely reported.

2. Report on the basic dimensions of the receivables asset:

   - *Risk.* Age profile, risk profile by credit score, and bad debt expense

   - *Turnover.* DSO actual versus best possible and cash collected

   - *Quality.* Billing quality index, level of clutter

   - *Cost.* Cost of accounts receivable management group as percent of revenue

   - *Service.* Cycle time of disputes and credit application turnaround

- *Other.* Specialized, such as deductions, unbilled accounts receivable, and so on

Metrics for deduction management include:

- Days of deductions outstanding (DDO)
- Age profile of open deductions (number and value)
- Percentage and dollar amount denied and collected

Metrics for unbilled receivables include:

- Days of unbilled receivables and days of billings outstanding (DBO) in lieu of DSO
- Age profile of unbilled receivables and total value

The four Best Practices for reporting key activities (operations) that drive results are:

1. Report weekly and live by it. Weekly operations reporting is designed for the supervisors and managers who have to produce results. The advantage of weekly (and in some cases daily) reporting is that it allows timely corrective action to be taken. Often we hear receivables management supervisors say that last month's results were not up to expectations. The critical advantage of weekly reporting is that when the reports indicate substandard results are developing, there is still time left in the month to implement corrective action. Exhibit 6.2 is an example of a weekly operations report (also known as an activity plan) for the collections function.

   The important characteristics to note about the collection activity plan are:

   - Only the key drivers of results are included in the "Inputs" section. Ask yourself: "What two to three actions or indicators do I need to monitor to know we are on track to meeting our targets this month?"

Exhibit 6.2 Collection Activity Plan

	200X			July, 200X					
	April	May	June	2–6	9–13	16–20	23–27	30,31	MTD Total
Calls									
Actual	5,222	7,277	5,672	1,075	1,428	1,530	1,688	608	6,329
Target	5,250	6,525	6,930	1,320	1,650	1,485	1,485	594	6,534
% reached	99.5	111.5	81.8	81.4	86.5	103.0	113.7	102.4	96.9
Promise to Pay									
Actual	$21.6	$20.5	$23.4	$1.6	$2.4	$7.2	$4.3	$2.8	$18.3
Target	$20.0	$24.0	$26.0	$4.0	$5.0	$5.0	$5.0	$2.0	$21.0
% reached	108.1	85.3	89.7	39.3	47.0	144.4	85.8	141.0	86.9
Disputes									
Identified	213	232	241	43	52	57	54	12	218
Resolved	N/A	153	177	54	62	59	60	27	262
Cash Collected									
Actual	$37.5	$30.8	$39.7	$5.4	$6.3	$10.2	$8.0	$11.4	$41.2
Target	$36.0	$40.0	$43.0	$8.3	$7.5	$7.2	$8.1	$3.9	$35.0
% reached	104.1	76.9	92.3	64.6	83.6	141.0	98.9	291.7	117.6
Credit Memos Issued									
Actual	$6.4	$11.8	$38.5	$0.0	$3.0	$0.3	$1.3	$2.4	$7.0
Target	$11.0	$18.0	$20.0	$0.0	$1.0	$2.0	$1.0	$4.0	$8.0
% reached	58.2	65.8	192.3	N/A	299.0	13.0	131.0	60.3	87.1
A/R >90									
Actual	$52.4	$54.0	$37.4	N/A	$40.5	38.5	37.4	35.7	35.7
Target	$48.0	$45.0	$49.0	N/A	$36.0	$35.0	34.0	33.0	33.0
% reached	91.6	83.3	131.0	N/A	89.0	90.0	90.8	92.5	92.5
Days Sales Outstanding									
Actual	N/A	N/A	103	N/A	N/A	N/A	N/A	N/A	94
Target	N/A	N/A	99	N/A	N/A	N/A	N/A	N/A	96

Row group labels (left margin): I N P U T (Calls, Promise to Pay, Disputes); O U T P U T (Cash Collected, Credit Memos Issued, A/R >90, Days Sales Outstanding)

155

- As mentioned, the collection activity plan is set up to monitor the weekly volumes of activities, to provide an early opportunity to implement corrective action. Some activities, such as collection calls and payment promises, should be monitored on a daily basis.

- The activity plan can be used as a planning tool. Start with the results you wish to achieve at month end, then ask: "What volumes of key activities need to be performed at which times during the month to deliver the results I am seeking?" Then plan those volumes of activities and arrange for the resources to execute.

- The collection activity plan also displays the volumes achieved in the prior three months for a quick comparison.

- The "Outputs" are the key results metrics to be achieved, such as cash collected, DSO, aging parameters, and so on.

- The activity plan can be compiled for individual employees or departments as well as an aggregate version.

2. Prepare similar activity plans for other functional areas, particularly in the support functions. Exhibit 6.3 illustrates an activity plan for the payment processing (or cash application) function.

3. To gain the most benefit from activity plans, tailor them to the function and the individual company. They should not exceed one sheet of paper. If they are longer, you are approaching overkill.

4. The other operating report is the Major Problem Account report. As its name suggests, this report lists the top 10 (but no more than 15) problem accounts with pertinent receivables data. Its purpose is to focus senior management attention on these accounts to enlist their help in clearing them. In our experience, it is unrealistic to expect a member of senior management to be effective in dealing with more than two or three problem accounts, so the report should be structured accordingly. If this report is reviewed at a semimonthly or monthly management meeting, it can be very effective in mobilizing assistance to clear the problems.

Exhibit 6.3 Cash Application Activity Plan

			200X December		200X January		Week 1		February Week 2		Week 3	
			#	$	#	$	#	$	#	$	#	$
I	Payments received (actual)				3,414	$2,279						
N												
D	Payments applied (actual)											
I	a. Autocash				2,547	$1,551						
C	b. Hit rate				75%	68%						
A	c. Manually—total				867	$728						
T												
O	Payments not applied											
R	Actual				*	$*						
S	Target				*	$*						

R	Unapplied cash	
E	Actual	$248
S	Target	$200
U	Unapplied cash ≥ 30 days old	
L	Actual	$151
T	Target	$50
S	Reapply requests received	
	Credit and adjustment backlog	$*

Note: Figures are actual.

INCENTIVES

Incentives can be extremely useful in motivating staff to achieve excellent performance. One of the critical qualifications for a good incentive plan is that it should be able to be objectively measured. Receivables management performance can be objectively measured and quickly, so rewards can be paid quickly. Delivering the reward as soon as possible after the desired behavior has been displayed is another basic principle of incentives.

Of all the functions within receivables management, collections is the one most conducive to effective incentives. The support functions are more difficult to measure and lend themselves better to group incentives based on throughput and quality.

Even with collection incentives, subjectivity and/or lack of equity issues can be raised with the setting of targets or with the allocation of accounts. These issues require attention to avoid neutralizing the incentive through establishing what are perceived as unattainable targets. However, no incentive scheme is ever beyond question. Receivables management is very compatible with incentives, especially when compared to other administrative functions.

Other important considerations for designing incentive plans for receivables management staff are:

- Do not include elements that must be subjectively evaluated. Save those for the annual performance review, and reward achievement of these elements through increases to the base salary.

- Keep it simple and easy-to-understand. Minimize the number of metrics on which the incentive is based. Minimize the amount of time required to administer the plan.

- Include group and individual rewards where appropriate. Incentives based on group achievements are excellent for supervisors. They are also useful for the support processing functions where teamwork is essential in handling overflow, filling in for absent coworkers, and so on.

► **CASE HISTORY** ◄

Dangers of Overcomplicating Incentive Strategy

A multibillion-dollar manufacturer of high-technology equipment designed an extremely complex incentive plan for its sales force. Over time, modifications made it even more complex. It was difficult to understand, reducing its motivational effect. In addition, it was extremely difficult to administer. A study revealed that it consumed the time of 400 full-time equivalents, plus substantial management time. The cost of this incentive plan was millions of dollars annually for motivation of limited value.

- Incentives can be used successfully with both staff and front-line supervisors.

- Pay the incentives monthly or at least quarterly. This increases motivation. Annual goals with annual payouts are not as effective in motivating daily performance. Also, if it becomes apparent in midyear that the annual target will not be achieved, performance can really suffer.

- Utilize graduated payouts over a narrow range of achievement. All-or-nothing payouts can be demotivating, especially when the shortfall is minor. Minor shortfalls also tempt management to make exceptions, which undermine the integrity of the target.

- Avoid negative or "clawback" incentives, which can be demoralizing. The worst-case outcome of an incentive plan should be zero payout, not a recapture of payouts previously disbursed.

- The amount of the incentive should be a significant percentage of the base salary, so it really means something. Incentives of 10 to 15% of base salary will win attention and motivate staff.

INCENTIVES BEST PRACTICES

Best Practices for incentive plans for collection staff incorporate the attributes described above. The best, simplest incentive for collections is actual cash collected versus a target. After all, you do not pay collectors to write receivables off, process credits, and shuffle paperwork. Cash collection is the primary mission. If the targets are set properly, achieving the cash target will enable achievement of virtually all the other quantitative results. DSO and aging will fall in line if cash collection goals are consistently met. The need to remove clutter and other aged uncollectables can be established as an objective to be evaluated in the annual performance review. Designing the collection incentive to depend on just one metric is the simplest-to-understand, easiest-to-administer incentive scheme. This incentive is most effective when it is an individual incentive. You may wish to add an extra payout when the overall cash target is met, but an individual incentive is the most effective means of motivating a collector. The critical task is setting individual targets that are achievable and realistic, not demotivating.

The best way to set realistic, achievable monthly cash collection targets for an individual collector is to:

- Start with the summary receivables by aging category for the prior month-end for the collector's assigned accounts.

- Identify major, troubled accounts (i.e., bankrupt, litigation, collection agency, embroiled in a major dispute, etc.) from whom you realistically cannot expect any significant payments. Exclude (subtract) them from the summary receivables.

- Quantify the amount of cash collections expected from each aging category. Use historical collection percentages if available, and remember to discount the expected cash by the prevailing incidence of disputes that will probably not result in cash in the upcoming month. If disputed invoices can be identified and quantified, exclude most of them from the summary aging, based on historical collection percentages.

- After all exclusions are made, and the expected percentage of cash is calculated for each aging category, sum for all categories for the total. This total is the cash collection target for the coming month.

- If a significant portion of sales are made on payment terms of less than 30 days, the cash from these sales must be computed from the sales forecast and added to the total cash target. Examples of such cash are credit, debit, or procurement card sales, cash-in-advance sales, down payments, and deposits.

Exhibit 6.4 provides an example of a cash collection target calculation.

Assuming a standard net 30-day payment term and $3 million of credit card sales, the cash collection target for the illustrative portfolio in Exhibit 6.4 is $39,200,000.

Remember, the ability to measure actual cash receipts by collector is essential to utilizing cash collection incentives. Nontrade receivable cash (i.e., royalty payments, asset sales, etc.) must be excluded.

Best Practices for incentive plans for support functions include the general attributes mentioned above. The incentive plans should be based on throughput and quality. A good metric for throughput is the magnitude and age of backlog. For example, the incentive plan for payment processing is best structured to payout on achievement of:

- Maintenance of the backlog of unapplied cash (both unidentified and unposted cash) consistently below a specified level. The target level should be equivalent to a fraction (one-half or one-third) of an average day's cash receipts. It should also include a condition reflecting age, such as no item unapplied more than 30 days beyond its receipt date or less than 10% of unapplied payments over 15 days from receipt date.

- Quality and accuracy standards. The best way to measure accuracy is the number of payments in the period that had to be reapplied (i.e., the original application reversed, and the payment reapplied). The tolerance for this quality metric should be extremely low, approaching zero. There are cases when a payment is applied correctly and has to be reapplied because the customer made an error. These types of reapplies are rare, so reapplies are a valid measure of first-time quality. Usually the

Exhibit 6.4 Sample Cash Collection Target Calculation (in $000)

	Current	Past Due 1 to 30	Past Due 31 to 60	Past Due 61 to 90	Past Due 91–Plus	Total
Beginning balance	$30,000	$10,000	$8,000	$4,000	$6,000	$58,000
Troubled accounts	(500)	(900)	(700)	(800)	(1,200)	(4,100)
Dispute dilution	(1,500)	(1,000)	(2,000)	(1,800)	(3,000)	(9,300)
Available to collect	28,000	8,100	5,300	1,400	1,800	44,600
Collection percent	79	85	87	86	83	81
Cash to be collected	22,000	6,900	4,600	1,200	1,500	36,200
Cash from current month sales	3,000					3,000
Cash target	$25,000	$6,900	$4,600	$1,200	$1,500	$39,200

reapplies will be so infrequent that they can be evaluated on a case-by-case basis to ensure they are error-based.

The incentive plan for a dispute resolution team would also be based on:

- Backlog (number and age based on the normal volume of incoming disputes and the standard resolution time established). For example, if 10 disputes are normally received each day, and the standard response time is 12 days, the backlog target could be set at 15 days' worth of disputes to allow for some slack in the system (or 150), with no dispute open more than 45 days.

- Cycle time from identification to resolution. In the above example, the cycle time target would be 15 days.

- Ultimate outcome. The ultimate outcome is defined as the manner in which the dispute is cleared from the receivables ledger. Disputes are cleared by noncash transactions (credit memos or adjustments), by cash payments, or by a combination of both. If a dispute resolution team is rewarded solely on clearing disputes fast and driving the backlog down, there is a bias to credit a dispute since this is a unilateral, fast way to clear it. Invalid disputes that should be collected from the customer may be credited in an effort to qualify for a backlog-only–based incentive. The measure of ultimate outcome serves as a check and balance on the bias to credit a dispute. The target for collecting disputes can be based on historical experience, but the percentage collected should increase over time for two reasons:

- Disputes should be addressed earlier in their life cycle. The earlier an invalid dispute is challenged with the customer, the greater the probability of collection.

- The continuous improvement efforts driven by dispute data should reduce the number of errors committed by your company, which in turn will decrease the number of disputes that should be credited.

KEY POINTS

Four points are key here:

1. Keep the incentive plan simple to minimize administration time, effort, and cost, and to make it easy to understand by all participants.

2. Set targets wisely. Targets should be set slightly higher than is required to achieve the overall department objectives.

3. Offer incentives for only those results that can be accurately and quickly measured, so payouts can be made quickly.

4. Ensure the amount of money is significant enough to merit attention to the incentive plan.

CHAPTER 7

Acquisition Integrations and ERP Implementations

OVERVIEW

Acquisition integrations and enterprise resource planning (ERP) implementations are two very different activities. Why are they grouped together in the same chapter? Both activities have a strong potential of negatively impacting receivables management results if not planned and executed properly. In addition, the methodology to recover from the negative receivables impact is similar for both initiatives.

The reason these initiatives impact receivables management results is that they affect the entire quote-to-cash process (i.e., the receivables antecedents described in Chapter 2). As explained in that chapter, any introduction of error or delay in the "upstream" processes will adversely impact the receivables asset. The chief manifestation of problems with the receivables antecedents is inaccurate invoices, which are extremely damaging to receivables management effectiveness and efficiency. The best way to illustrate this effect is with case histories.

Reading these case histories begs the question: How does this happen? First of all, integrating an acquisition and implementing a new ERP system are not easy tasks. They are major tasks requiring many months and the work of dozens if not hundreds of people, and it all

CASE HISTORY ◀

Examples of the High Costs to Receivables When Acquisitions or ERP Implementations Do Not Go Smoothly

Case One

A distributor of high-technology industrial supplies acquired a competitor approximately half its size. Both companies were high-transaction volume suppliers with tens of thousands of customers. In integrating the order entry, invoicing, and receivables management functions, it did not accurately transfer the acquired company's customer contract files. These files governed the product pricing for each major customer. As a result, thousands of incorrect invoices were issued. Customers either refused to pay the inaccurate invoices or short paid them, thereby producing thousands of deductions and disputes. The impact on the acquiring company was devastating. Six months after commencing order processing and invoicing for the combined enterprise:

- Seriously past due receivables (defined as over 150 days past due) tripled, increasing to $48 million.
- There were 150,000 open items aged beyond 150 days past due.
- 25,000 customer accounts had at least one item over 150 days past due.

The work and expense required to recover from this situation was enormous:

- It was nine months before receivables returned to the preacquisition aging profile.
- Over 40% of the receivables over 150 days past due ($19 million) were credited or written off.
- The cost of the recovery effort in extra labor and overtime was almost $500,000.

Case Two

A manufacturer of precision components integrated an acquisition and implemented a new ERP application simultaneously. These initiatives overloaded the organization's capability to implement change. The new ERP system would randomly default to list price when invoicing (very few customers paid list price), generating hundreds of inaccurate invoices. It deleteriously affected receivables management results:

Case History *(continued)*

- DSO increased by 31%, reducing cash flow by $30 million.
- The number of disputed invoices quadrupled.
- Customer service and credit and collection staffs were over-whelmed with the work required to resolve the huge volume of disputed invoices.
- Customer satisfaction was impacted.

The recovery from these problems:

- Required seven months of intensive effort.
- Cost over $650,000 in out-of-pocket extra help.
- Required issuing credit memos at triple the normal rate for over eight months.

Case Three

A capital equipment manufacturer acquired a competitor about one-third its size. It executed the integration of the order processing, ful-fillment, and invoicing fairly well as it combined the two firms' operations. It did not orchestrate the management of the acquired receivables well. Unwilling to add to the workload of its receivables management group or to incur additional expense, it assigned the responsibility for collecting the acquired receivables to a financial analysis department in corporate headquarters. This group was not trained in collections, nor did the staff members have a desire to learn collections. The results were disastrous. The acquired receiv-ables asset was reduced moderately during the one year it was administered by the corporate group. However, disputed and difficult-to-collect receivables remained open and were another year older. The organization and completeness of the files deteriorated during the year. By the time the acquiring firm's management real-ized the corporate group was not effective, they were faced with these problems:

- There were $6.1 million of open receivables aged between 15 months and 3 years.
- The $6.1 million was composed of almost 18,000 open items (invoices and many clutter transactions), with an average net value of $339.
- The files were missing numerous documents (proof of deliv-ery, purchase order, service reports, etc.).

(continues)

Case History *(continued)*

- The company was facing substantial write-offs and a significant expense to try to collect as much of the $6.1 million as
  possible.

Case Four
A medical insurance company implemented a new ERP system and
did not fully test the invoicing function. It initiated use of the new
system and discovered it could not generate invoices. It was assured
by the vendor that the problem was temporary and invoicing would
be operational in a few days. The insurer was unable to invoice for
two months. The impact on cash flow was disastrous even after invoicing was restored as customers balked at paying three monthly
premium invoices simultaneously. Many customers demanded extra
time to research their files to ensure the newly arrived invoices were
not duplicates. Other customers did not have the cash flow to pay all
of the invoices at once. The cost of borrowing to compensate for the
cash shortfall was hundreds of thousands of dollars.

Case Five
Similar invoicing problems were encountered during an ERP implementation by a production equipment manufacturer that was unable to invoice for seven weeks. A similar impact was experienced
with cash flow.

Case Six
A software developer implemented a new ERP system with difficulty.
One year after activating the invoicing function, it was discovered
that over $3 million of maintenance and support invoices were never
generated. It developed a special approach to collecting these receivables, which included training for sales, customer service, as well
as collections. The firm generated and mailed the invoices, but had
to incur extra expense and time to collect them.

must be coordinated through a project management function. However, two common mistakes contribute to problems with these initiatives. They are:

1. Inadequate resources, especially:

- Functional expertise in the quote-to-cash and receivables management processes.

- Information technology (IT) expertise.

- Supplemental resources. Staff members are needed to continue to process the normal flow of work, to assist in the integration or implementation, and to clean up the receivables portfolio before it is integrated or converted to the new system. Often, supplemental resources are not sufficient for the work needed.

- Senior management resources to drive results and secure resources as needed.

2. Inadequate planning of the tasks required. The task most frequently under- or poorly planned is the preparation of the:

   - Existing receivables portfolio for conversion to the new ERP system.

   - Acquired receivables portfolio for integration into the acquiring company's receivable management infrastructure. The receivables management staff of an acquired company will usually realize their jobs will be terminated when the receivables management function is consolidated into the acquiring company. As a result, their performance will often be inadequate to clean up the portfolio as needed prior to consolidation. Even with incentives, the staff turnover and lagging performance may not be sufficient to prepare the portfolio as planned.

As the case histories illustrate, the impact of a poorly executed acquisition integration or system conversion can result in:

- Ultimate loss of the acquired or converted portfolio of up to 10% of its value through bad debt or concessions

- Seriously decreased cash flow in the short and medium term

- Substantial extra cost to recover from the effects of the poor execution (overtime, temporary help)

- Damaged customer satisfaction

BEST PRACTICES

For the purpose of our Best Practices for integrating an acquired receivables portfolio and/or implementing a new ERP system, we will restrict the scope to only those critical steps that affect the receivables asset. Acquisition integration and ERP implementation each merit a separate book.

The three major areas critical to the successful acquisition integration or systems conversion of a receivables portfolio are:

1. Planning and execution
2. Portfolio cleanup
3. Recovering from suboptimal execution

Planning and Execution

Plan the new quote-to-cash process work flow from end to end. For each step, plan the source of required information, what the information inputs and outputs will be, and the processing to be performed. Ensure the system functionality can perform as needed and test, test, test. For acquisitions:

- Ensure the product numbers for the products of the acquired company are loaded into the product master files in acceptable formats, and do not duplicate existing product numbers.

- Ensure the customer numbers for the acquired customers do not duplicate existing ones. The truly new ones must be loaded into the customer master files in the proper format. Retain the existing credit limits and update the riskier ones as soon as possible.

- Ensure the pricing files and contracts for newly acquired customers are in place.

- If information is to be retrieved from the acquired company's system on an ongoing basis, ensure the interfaces are built properly to enable the retrieval.

- Retain the acquired company's lockbox. Even if you communicate a change in lockbox and remittance address to customers, it will take months and continuous reminders to get all customers to use the new lockbox address.

- Mail an official communication to the acquired company's customers announcing the acquisition and listing contact names and phone numbers, the correct payee name, and the correct remittance address. This letter is best signed by executives from both the acquired and acquiring company to add credibility to the announcement.

- Transfer all electronic and hard-copy files pertaining to current customers and open receivables. This includes collection notes for the past 6 to 12 months stored in the acquired company's collection application as well as hard copies or images of invoices, purchase orders, proofs of delivery, checks and their application, and so on. Ensure the files are in proper order to facilitate quick retrieval.

- Retain a few members of the acquired company's receivables management group if possible. They will bring a wealth of information about the new customers. Arrange an account-by-account briefing between the outgoing collection staff of the acquired company and the team taking over. Similarly, secure a thorough understanding of the acquired company's payment processing procedures and files.

- Set a cutoff date for when all orders will be handled by the new consolidated system and staff. Ensure the invoicing will be handled by the consolidated system and the receivables and payments posted to the new receivables ledger.

- If at all possible, maintain the "pre-cutoff" receivables on a separate legacy application (the acquired company's receivables ledger). By using a separate application, no new invoices will be added. The receivables balance will decrease only through application of payments, credit memos, adjustments, and so on. Utilization of the separate ledger facilitates the deployment of a temporary team. It enables them to focus on only the receivables they must clear. In addition, measurement is easy.

Portfolio Cleanup

The principle of portfolio cleanup is simple: It is easier to integrate or convert a smaller, less complex receivables portfolio than it is a large, disorganized, complex one. The way to achieve a smaller, less complex portfolio is to clear as many of the open items as possible.

Perfection in a receivables portfolio to be converted or integrated is to have it composed exclusively of current, whole open invoices. This is the ideal state. In practice, it is not achievable without incurring substantial, unnecessary write-offs. Think about what the perfect portfolio *does not* contain:

- Past due invoices
- Deductions (or short payments)
- Unapplied cash
- Unapplied credit memos
- Open chargebacks
- Unearned discounts
- Late payment fees

All but the first transaction type are also known as clutter. While in the real world it is not possible to clear all of these open transactions, the more that are cleared, the easier the integration and/or conversion. Remember, the collectability of these transactions is diminished. The work required to collect them is great. Passing clutter on to the new consolidated receivables management group or to the new system will make the task of managing the new work flow much more difficult. This is another reason for leaving "pre-cutoff" or "pre-cut-over" receivables on a separate ledger. That way, they can be worked until cleared or wither on the vine without impacting the new system or receivables management team.

Retaining the collection staff of the acquired company with an incentive for staying until the end, or utilizing temporary resources, is an excellent way to clean up a portfolio. When the job is finished, the resource and expense is discontinued. Remember, a full staff is needed to deal with the ongoing business volume. A special effort to clean up the portfolio merits additional resource.

Recovering from Suboptimal Execution

If the planning, execution, and portfolio cleanup still leave you with an increase in past due receivables and a decrease in cash flow, the high-impact action program and the reconciliation and recovery program described in Chapter 3 under "Special Collection Efforts" have proven to be excellent tools for rebounding from the disruption. These tools can enable you to liquidate work backlogs and restore the receivables asset to the desired condition. At this point, the normal operations of the receivables management group should be sufficient to achieve the desired results. Exhibits 7.1, 7.2, and 7.3 illustrate how effective these tools can be in recovering from a faulty acquisition integration.

Exhibit 7.1   Recovery from Acquisition Integration Problems

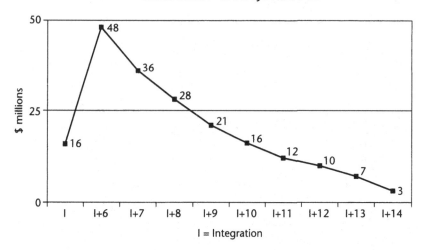

Acquisition integration case study
Receivables > 150 Days Past Due

I = Integration

Exhibit 7.2   Recovery from Acquisition Integration Problems

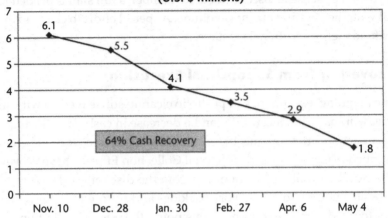

Capital Equipment Client
Seriously Aged Service Receivables Portfolio
(U.S. $ millions)

Exhibit 7.3   Recovery from Acquisition Integration Problems

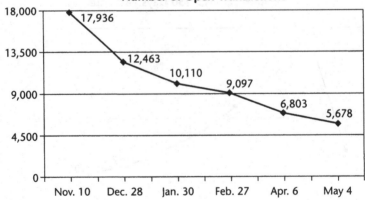

Capital Equipment Client
Seriously Aged Service Receivables Portfolio
Number of Open Transactions

KEY POINTS

The four key points to remember about integrating an acquired receivables portfolio or converting it to a new ERP system are:

1. Plan thoroughly for the move.

2. Provide adequate resources, both functional and information technology, to process ongoing business, plan and execute the move, and clean up the receivables portfolio prior to the conversion/integration.

3. Clean up the portfolio before integrating or converting it. Better yet, segregate and track it on a separate receivables ledger.

4. If receivables results are still impacted, utilize a high-impact action and/or reconciliation and recovery program to restore the asset to the desired condition.

CHAPTER 8

Outsourcing

OVERVIEW

Outsourcing is the action of hiring an outside firm to perform designated functions. The trend toward outsourcing business functions is well established and is gaining momentum across a wide range of industries. Human resource administration, warehousing, order fulfillment, call centers, and application programming are examples of functions commonly outsourced. In fact, the issue of outsourcing functions to overseas locations has become a political issue in the United States that was debated during the 2004 presidential election.

Outsourcing is usually performed two ways:

1. Functions are outsourced to the outsourcer's off-site processing center. The outsourcer performs the function with its staff using its information technology (IT) system. Connectivity to the outsourcing company's IT system is essential for this arrangement to work.

2. The outsourcer performs the function on-site in the outsourcing company's office. The outsourcer still provides the staff and management, and may use its IT application or the outsourcing company's application.

Receivables management, specifically the credit, collection, and payment processing functions, are likely candidates for outsourcing, when a company believes one or more of these reasons apply:

- The functions are not considered a core competency.

- The functions can be performed for lower cost by an outsourcer.

- The outsourcers are specialists and can achieve better results in improving cash flow and bad debt exposure.

- The outsourcing company can avoid capital investment in IT designed to support the credit, collection, and payment processing functions.

It should be noted that there is a big difference between outsourcing the complete collection function for all or a portion of customer accounts and using a collection agency. Outsourcing commits the outsourcer to work the entire customer account including current and recently past due amounts. A collection agency usually receives only uncooperative, seriously past due accounts that have been cut off from shipments or service.

The growth of outsourcing credit, collection, and payment processing is testimony to its ability to deliver cost and performance improvements. However, outsourcing is not for everyone. It has to be executed properly to generate the benefits expected. The outsourcing company cannot totally wash its hands of the functions. It must:

- Provide a significant level of support to the outsourcer

- Expend effort in monitoring the outsourcer's performance

- Monitor their customers' reaction to the outsourcer's contact

---

▶ CASE HISTORY ◀

Two Outsourcing Failures

While there are many successful outsourcing case studies, these two illustrate outsourcing failures.

Case One

A high-tech company outsourced its credit, collection, and payment processing functions to the off-site facility of a large, well-known professional services firm. After six months, the receivables manage-

Case History *(continued)*

ment results had deteriorated, and the outsourcing agreement was terminated. The failure was caused by both parties.

The outsourcing company:

- Had poor-quality billing, which generated a high volume of disputes.
- Lacked a formal dispute resolution process. The roles of the outsourcer and the client were undefined.
- Responded slowly or not at all to the outsourcer's inquiries for help with disputes.
- Responded slowly to decisions on escalating collection efforts with uncooperative customers.

The outsourcer:

- Was new to the field of receivables process outsourcing.
- Staffed its team with inexperienced personnel.
- Managed the team with supervisors who were experienced in business process redesign, but not credit and collection tactics.
- Failed to design and agree to a formal dispute management process with the client prior to commencing the outsourcing processing.

Case Two

The second case concerns a consumer products manufacturer that incurred a high volume of deductions and outsourced its collection and deductions processing to the off-site facility of a leading accounts receivable outsourcing firm. It retained the credit and payment processing functions in-house. After only five months, receivables management results had deteriorated, and the outsourcing agreement was terminated. Here again, the failure was caused by both parties.

The outsourcing company:

- Failed to provide many of the debit memos and other documents supplied by customers in support of deductions to the outsourcer. Many of the documents were missing.
- Failed to supply the outsourcer with information documenting promotional discounts offered their customers. Most of the deductions taken by customers were valid, as they were

(continues)

> **Case History** *(continued)*
>
> consistent with the promotions offered. The outsourcer did
> not have the information required to efficiently clear the valid
> deductions.
> - Did not render timely decisions on disputes that required a
>   management decision to resolve.
> - Did not respond to requests for information regarding dis-
>   putes on a timely basis.
>
> The outsourcer:
> - Understaffed the collection function by 50%. The delinquency
>   of open invoices deteriorated as a result.
> - Failed to be proactive in securing necessary information from
>   the client.
> - Failed to escalate the inadequate cooperation it was receiving
>   from the client to the client's senior management.

BEST PRACTICES

Best Practices for outsourcing some or all of the receivables management function start with the decision to outsource or keep some or all
of the functions in-house. Making the right decision is critical. If a decision is made to use an outsourcer, then the organization must commit
to support the outsourcer properly or optimal value will not be
achieved. A company cannot completely wash its hands of these vital
operations.

Answering these six questions will enable the right decision for your
organization.

1. *Should we outsource our entire customer base or a portion of it?* Outsourcing the entire customer base would probably be the most
   cost effective and save the most management time. However, it
   may not be the best way to handle your larger, key customers
   from which you derive the most revenue and profit and to
   which you have the most credit risk exposure. Remember, credit

and collection helps your customers maintain their accounts with you in good order, thereby facilitating immediate fulfillment of their orders. That is why some firms call their credit and collections departments customer financial services.

Portions of the customer base more conducive to outsourcing are the international customers (especially Europe, with its relatively fragmented markets, each with a language requirement) and your smaller customers. *Caveat: Ensure your "small" customers are truly small, not just customers with a low receivable balance on the day you categorize them.*

2. *Which functions should be outsourced?* Outsourcing all functions can be the most cost efficient and most management time efficient. Operations most conducive to outsourcing are payment processing (combined with lockbox processing and auto-cash), credit scoring, and high-volume collections of smaller accounts. Collections on larger accounts and dispute and deduction processing are more complex and require much higher levels of support to the outsourcer, so the labor savings will be lower.

3. *Are you prepared to properly support the outsourcer?* As stated earlier, you cannot completely wash your hands of these critical functions. Shortcomings on your part could severely impair the effectiveness of the outsourcer. Examples of such shortcomings are:

   a. Poor systems interface with the outsourcer's applications

   b. Poor billing, order fulfillment, and/or service quality

   In addition, there will be a need for active, ongoing support to provide:

   a. Direction to enforce the credit policies the outsourcer is administering

   b. Requested information promptly to quickly resolve customer disputes and deductions

   c. Timely management decisions on exceptions, escalations, and when there are gray areas

Finally, there is a large, up-front set of tasks to equip the outsourcer with the tools, information, and empowerment required to perform the functions excellently. Regardless of which receivables management functions are outsourced, these setup tasks will be required:

d. Complete systems compatibility and interconnectivity to enable two-way information flow, communication, and processing to be exchanged. This is always more difficult than initially envisioned. Online processing is preferable to overnight batch processing.

e. Providing the outsourcer access to the hard copy and electronic files needed. This may include customer master files, contracts, pricing, shipping, invoicing, sales orders, returns, marketing promotions, and so on as well as the receivables and payment posting applications.

f. Agreeing on the process and work flows for the functions to be outsourced, including who performs which steps and overall roles and responsibilities. Examples of these processes are the collection timeline with escalation protocol, dispute resolution, deduction processing, and unapplied cash handling.

g. Empowerment for the outsourcer to negotiate and settle with a customer, with unilateral adjustment thresholds.

4. *Is the outsourcer competent?* Does the firm have the technical and human resources, industry experience, and experience with a company of your size and portfolio dimensions (i.e., 20 customers who owe you $15 million each versus 5 million customers who owe you $300 each)? Check multiple references and do a walk-through of the outsourcer's facility.

5. *Are you confident the outsourcer will treat your key customers right?* If it does not, your competitor will. Do not forget the customer service aspects of receivables management. It fosters frequent contact with customers, and the state of the customer's account is a good barometer of the quality of service being provided.

Getting close to your major customers through face-to-face visits builds rapport and relationships.

6. *If you position your company to properly support the outsourcer, should you just do the rest in-house?* When the systems are operating properly, your order fulfillment/billing/service quality is strong, and your dispute process is robust, you have done the heavy lifting. At that point, the classic credit and collection function may not be that difficult or costly.

If the decision has been made to outsource some or all of the receivables management functions, the next major step of Best Practices is to find an outsourcer and finalize a service-level agreement (SLA) with the outsourcer.

Finding an outsourcer, like finding any service or product provider, is best accomplished through a competitive bidding process. Enlist the aid of the procurement department to help get the best deal. Candidates should be selected from among outsourcers who have experience in your industry and with companies of your size. Solicit and interview references, and conduct a walk-through of the outsourcer's facility. Then narrow the list of candidates down to three, and ask for quotations.

Negotiation and contract writing is a science in itself, but here are six helpful tips for constructing the SLA:

1. Familiarize yourself with the transaction volumes in the functions to be outsourced. The cost of the service will be based, in part, on the volumes. Know the seasonal peak volumes, the lows, and the average or "run rate," and how the volumes may change during the term of the agreement.

2. If outsourcing the collection function, use the collection call intensity options model (see Exhibit 5.1) to decide how intensely you wish the receivables portfolio to be worked. The intensity chosen will determine the volume of collection calls required and the staff level the outsourcer will need.

3. Beware one-time setup costs, à la carte pricing, and cost escalators.

4. Do not begrudge the outsourcer a profit on the deal. The out-
    sourcer will make a profit eventually, and an extremely low
    price will force the outsourcer to reduce resource and service to
    you and your customers. Remember, this is a partnership where
    the outsourcer will share your systems and interact with your
    employees and your *customers.*

5. Ensure the work flows and roles and responsibilities for each
    function are clearly documented and incorporated into the con-
    tract.

6. Define the communication flows and issue resolution protocols
    between outsourcer and your firm.

The last major dimension of outsourcing is monitoring the results of
the outsourcing arrangement. The receivables management results can
be monitored using the techniques outlined in Chapter 6 of this book.
You can even get the outsourcer to produce most of the metrics and reporting, but always *verify the results independently.*

The cost of the arrangement is easily tracked through your accounts
payable records. The actual cost can be compared to the SLA and the internal budget for the function.

The quality of service and impact on your customers can be tracked
two ways:

1. By commissioning a polling firm that specializes in customer
    satisfaction studies to conduct a statistically significant poll of
    your customer base

2. By regularly questioning your sales force and customer service
    groups for feedback they have received from customers regard-
    ing the outsourced functions

Diligence in monitoring results is critically important to ensuring the
outsourcing agreement delivers the results and efficiencies expected.

KEY POINTS

There are three key points regarding outsourcing:

1. Outsourcing works for many companies and fails for others. The decision to outsource at all, and then the determination of which functions, is critically important. Devote the proper amount of time and effort to the decision.

2. Find the right outsourcer through intensive investigation and competitive bidding. Then partner with the firm; do not treat it as an adversary.

3. Measure and monitor results and costs.

CHAPTER 9

Selected Topics

INTRODUCTION

This chapter provides brief comments on other receivables asset management topics.

POLICY AND PROCEDURES

Policies and procedures for each of the functions within receivables management are very important. Policies document management's formal posture on each function (e.g., credit policy addresses risk tolerance). Procedures delineate the actions and steps to be taken for each operation.

Clear policies are required as part of strong internal controls, which we will discuss in more detail in the next section. They also provide guidance to employees charged with performing the functions. Inevitably, employees will be faced with decisions that are not explicitly covered by detailed procedures. In these instances, acting in concurrence with the governing policy will usually be judged the proper decision.

Detailed procedures contribute to receivables management effectiveness and efficiency in two major ways:

1. They serve as a reference for experienced employees in performing their job functions.

2. They are excellent tools for initial and refresher training of newer employees.

Detailed procedures are also required as part of strong internal controls.

Best Practice is for policy and procedures to be stored online with read-only access granted to anybody who may need to refer to them. Online storage facilitates revisions and updates. Access to revise the policies and procedures must be restricted to a few individuals, and any changes must be approved by authorized individuals.

Policies and procedures should be reviewed periodically (the external auditors can advise how frequently) and updated as needed.

INTERNAL CONTROLS

As stated, the existence and compliance with policies and detailed procedures are a fundamental requirement of strong internal controls. Even prior to the passage of the Sarbanes-Oxley Act of 2002, strong internal controls were vital to all companies, but especially publicly owned companies. External auditors would refuse to attest to the financial statements of companies whose internal controls were inadequate. Internal controls are also important for the protection of a company's assets. Numerous cases have been identified where embezzlement or fraud was perpetrated involving billing, returned goods, cash application, and receivables. The absence of effective internal controls would expose a company to a high level of risk of loss from fraud.

With the advent of Sarbanes-Oxley, the need for strong internal controls has intensified because of the civil and criminal penalties and the increased scrutiny of oversight organizations. One area of major focus of Sarbanes-Oxley is not the safeguarding of company assets but the accuracy of financial reporting. Under Sarbanes-Oxley, companies must document their procedures and the flow of financial information that feeds their financial reporting. As a result, policies and procedures governing receivables management are more important than ever.

Receivables-related issues can pose a risk to the accuracy and reliability of financial statements. The receivables asset and revenue can be overstated, and expenses understated, by the existence of a significant level of uncollectable receivables on the balance sheet. The clearing of those uncollectables will decrease revenue if cleared by a debit to revenue (credit memo or adjustment) and increase expenses if cleared by a write-off to bad debt. Unless effective procedures are in place to clear and/or reserve adequately for uncollectables, there is a risk that the financial statements will be inaccurate.

The passage of Sarbanes-Oxley has increased the need for sound policies and procedures that are an integral part of internal controls.

A list of internal controls over the revenue cycle and the receivables asset can be found in an auditing textbook.

FINANCING OF THE RECEIVABLES ASSET

There are various techniques for using the receivables asset to obtain accelerated funding instead of waiting for customers to pay the invoices. All of these techniques:

- Involve an incremental financing or borrowing cost
- Impose duties and restrictions on the borrower
- Are structured differently

Since they are all financing instruments with a high degree of customization, they must be evaluated very carefully and negotiated with the lender. **It is highly recommended that the advice of an impartial receivables funding, treasury, or financing expert be utilized in negotiating and structuring any financing agreement.**

A brief description of the various types of receivables funding follows.

Sale of Receivables

This is the simplest form of financing, where a company sells its receivables asset to a financing entity. The financing entity takes title to the asset and pays a lump sum in return. Of course, the seller does not receive 100 cents for every dollar of receivables sold. The purchase price is reduced for:

- The interest value of the money advanced by the buyer. The rate is based on prevailing interest rates, the length of time the lender expects to wait before receiving payment for all invoices purchased, and the risk premium the lender perceives for the risk of nonpayment of the purchased receivables.

- Expected dilution (deductions, discounts, etc.) incurred in collecting the receivables.

- The cost to the buyer of collecting the receivables. Since the receivables have been sold to the buyer, the buyer will have to collect them. Usually, the seller mails a letter to customers informing them of the assignment of the receivables to the buyer and how to pay (payee name, address).

- A profit element.

In addition, the buyer may not purchase all of the receivables offered. The buyer may eliminate receivables owed by high-risk customers, either individual customers or a class of customers, such as foreign accounts.

The advantage to the seller is that it receives the funds in a matter of days instead of waiting 30 or more days. However, this can be an expensive way to obtain financing.

Factoring Receivables

Factoring of receivables is very similar to the sale technique described above. The major difference is that factoring is a continuous, ongoing purchase of receivables, compared to a transaction for a finite portfolio of receivables.

The factor serves as the seller's receivables management function, performing credit, collection, and payment processing functions. However, the factor will purchase receivables from only customers whose creditworthiness has been vetted and approved. If the seller sells to customers not accepted to the factor, the seller has to perform the receivables management function itself.

Collateralizing Receivables

Collateralizing receivables involves pledging the asset as collateral for a loan. The simplest form is pledging them as a condition for obtaining a term loan. The company continues to administer them as always, except there will be covenants specifying standards of aging, concentration, and so on to be met, and reporting requirements from the lender. Often the lender will exclude receivables over 90 days past due and expected dilution from the collateral valuation and reduce the amount financed. For example, the receivables ledger may show a face value of $100 million, but only $80 million may accepted as collateral by the lender.

Another form of collateralization is securitization, where the receivables asset is used to secure commercial paper or other financing instrument issued to third-party investors. Securitization is an ongoing financing instrument with acceptable receivables purchased by the financing entity on a continuous basis. The seller manages the asset as always, but with additional procedural and reporting duties and covenants.

The cost of all of these financing techniques is inversely related to the quality of the receivables asset. The discount or interest rate used will be based on the factors described in the "Sale of Receivables" section. Evaluation of the cost involves two key elements:

1. The cost of the funds obtained through receivables financing compared to the cost of funds obtained through other financing techniques

2. The cost of managing the receivables asset and complying with the financing entity's requirements compared to the cost of managing the asset without receivables financing arrangements

Financing receivables is often used when other financing sources are unavailable or exhausted. It is difficult to justify incurring significant costs to receive the cash from receivables 30 to 50 days earlier. Remember, when receivables are financed, it is usually most or all of the asset. This includes numerous customers who pay on time or close to it. As a result, financing costs are incurred on a revenue stream that converts to cash in 30 to 40 days.

In conclusion, the financing of receivables can be an important source of funds, but it can be expensive and should be evaluated carefully.

PAYMENT TERM CHANGES

Changing payment terms is an important senior management decision that has strategic implications. Payment terms directly affect the level of investment in receivables (which is among the three largest assets for most companies). Payment terms are an integral part of the price and can affect customer retention. Payment terms are difficult to change. If a change in terms is contemplated, consider the fact that:

- Increasing terms will raise the investment in receivables and reduce cash flow. If not granted to similar categories of customers, it may expose a company to price discrimination charges. It is difficult to decrease terms once extended.

- Decreasing terms will reduce the investment in receivables and improve cash flow. However, it is very difficult to accomplish. In our experience, it will require senior management to deliver the message to key customers. Customers will usually ask for a price reduction or an increased prompt payment discount. Terms reductions are best implemented during an announced price increase, when the amount of increase can be diminished somewhat in exchange for faster payments.

Receivables Management Success Stories

CASE STUDY ONE

SOFTWARE DEVELOPER

The Company

The company is a software developer whose product enables small and midsize financial services firms to automate their businesses. Its revenue stream includes license fees, installation, training, technical support, and hardware. The complexity of new product offerings, strong growth, and staff turnover all contributed to a deterioration of receivables management results. As the aging profile worsened (over 50% of receivables were more than 60 days past due) and bad debt exposure and expense increased, management designated improved receivables management as a top priority.

The Solution

The work team assigned the task assessed the processes and the state of the receivables portfolio. The work team determined which practices were sound and built on them, while redesigning other procedures to improve effectiveness. The key elements of this solution were:

- A redesigned portfolio strategy that focused the majority of effort on the 9% of customers that owed over 90% of the receivables asset, while controlling the thousands of small accounts that constituted a serious bad debt risk.

- A high-volume collection calling effort on the larger accounts. Collection training enhanced this effort.

- Establishing weekly targets for each collector for both key activities and results. Reporting actual results versus tar-

(continues)

gets enabled staff members to monitor their progress and provided an objective basis for evaluating their performance.

- Frequent performance reviews of collection staff members to provide feedback and improve their effectiveness.

- A collection letter routine directed at the thousands of small-balance accounts.

- A reconciliation and recovery effort focused on large accounts with disputed and "cluttered" balances.

The Results

In six months, the following results were achieved:

- A 54% reduction in the over-90-day past-due receivables
- A 49% reduction in total past-due receivables
- A reduction in bad debt expense of 45%
- DSO reduction of over 30 days.

With the process changes that were implemented, these results will be sustained—and advanced. The performance metrics developed will enable management to monitor progress and take corrective action when necessary. The client has since reduced its DSO to below 40 days.

CASE STUDY TWO

MAJOR SOFTWARE COMPANY

The Company

The company is a major software company. It was seeking improved receivables management by bringing its outsourced credit and collection functions back in-house. Poor management of the receivables asset had resulted in decreased cash flow, deteriorating aging, and a declining stock price. The company's immediate priorities were to:

- Arrest the deteriorating results and drive improvement
- Orchestrate the transition from the outsourcer and establish an in-house credit and collection operation

The Solution

The project team quickly assessed the receivables portfolio and the existing receivables management processes and designed an action plan to accomplish the above-mentioned objectives. It deployed a team of three senior supervisors to drive critical segments of the project during the succeeding six months, which included:

- Design of a portfolio strategy and collection process to maximize cash flow.
- Recruitment, training, and direct day-to-day management of a transition collection team.
- Development of an escalation protocol and an ad hoc dispute management process.

(continues)

CASE STUDY TWO *(continued)*

- Institution of weekly activity and results targets with reporting of achievement.

- Design of the organizational structure of the in-house Credit and Collection Department, specifying number and required skill set of staff, and their roles and responsibilities. Trained new staff as they were hired.

- An orderly phased transition of functions from transitory staff to the permanent staff.

The Results

- Cash receipts increased 22% on a constant revenue level in the first full quarter of the project compared to the prior quarter.

- Days Sales Outstanding (DSO) decreased 42% from prior year levels, releasing the equivalent of $55 million of cash from the receivables asset.

The stock price, aided by increased profitability, doubled in less than a year.

CASE STUDY THREE

MEDICAL PRODUCTS MANUFACTURER

The Company

The company is a medical products manufacturer that sells directly to hospitals. The company was experiencing a rapidly growing receivables asset, with a severe aging profile and substantial exposure to bad debt loss. This condition was the result of two "sea change" events:

1. The assimilation of a major acquisition

2. The implementation of a new ERP system

The Solution

A task force was organized to reverse the asset deterioration, increase cash flow, and reduce the exposure to bad debt loss. After a quick assessment of the receivables portfolio and revenue management processes, the task force formulated and implemented the following solution:

- Developed a portfolio strategy and redesigned the credit and collection management process to execute the strategy

- Provided an interim department manager to drive results, manage the staff, and ensure the new process was adopted and effectively performed

- Initiated a Reconciliation and Recovery effort for 150 aged, "cluttered" customer accounts

- Implemented a basic dispute management process

- Instituted activity and result targets and reporting of

(continues)

progress toward achieving the targets on a daily, weekly, and monthly basis

The Results

After six months, the company achieved the following results:

Indicator	Start	Finish	Percent Change
Days sales outstanding	63	49	(22)
> 90 day past due receivables*	$19	$7	(63)
Total receivables*	$111	$88	(21)
Percent of open transactions	76,000	49,000	(36)
Unapplied cash*	$1.6	$0.5	(69)

*In millions

In the final phase, the task force designed an organizational structure for the Credit department, specifying the number and skill sets of staff required to effectively manage the asset. The task force then managed the transition into the new organization, training new supervisors and staff, so the improvements achieved could be sustained and advanced. This client's DSO is consistently in the low 40 day range, and reached 37 in the summer of 2004.

CASE STUDY FOUR

ORTHOPEDIC THERAPY DEVICE MANUFACTURER

The Company

The company is a prominent manufacturer of orthopedic therapy devices selling to over 10,000 healthcare providers and distributors in the United States and overseas. Its operations were complicated by rapid growth, the integration of a major acquisition, and the implementation of a new ERP system. These events produced an escalating investment in receivables, a decrease in cash flow, and an increasing exposure to bad debt loss.

The Solution

A project team was formed to reverse the deterioration of the receivables asset and increase cash flow. Within three weeks it had analyzed the processes and the receivables asset and developed an action plan, which included:

- Development of a portfolio strategy and a redesigned collection process featuring streamlined workflows to free up more time for calls, advanced timing of calls, and weekly portfolio reviews

- A reorganization of the Credit Department including reallocation of accounts and redeployment of staff to handle the extreme volume of incoming calls, and provide administrative support to the collectors

- An upgrade of the staff's skills through refresher training on the system tools, and advanced collection and negotiation education

(continues)

CASE STUDY FOUR *(continued)*

- Institution of both activity and result tracking and reporting on a daily, weekly, and monthly basis

The Results

After only three months, average daily cash receipts increased by 33%, setting numerous records for daily, weekly, and monthly cash collections.

The increased cash was an indicator of the improvement in the underlying processes, people skills, and organization. The new metrics enabled management to monitor the progress with a minimal investment of time.

CASE STUDY FIVE

MEDICAL TEST EQUIPMENT SUPPLIER

The Company

The company is a leading worldwide supplier of medical test equipment selling to hospitals, laboratories, and government entities. The company was reducing its delinquent receivables at a steady rate but wished to accelerate progress in the short term.

The Solution

A dedicated team was formed to deliver accelerated delinquency reduction on a segment of the receivables portfolio comprised of 450 accounts controlling $23 million of receivables in a two-month time frame. To accomplish this, the team designed a high-impact action program, which includes only those actions and techniques that can be implemented within several weeks, and which are proven to begin delivering results within a month. Among the actions implemented were:

- A portfolio strategy designed to concentrate maximum focus on the high-yield segments
- Coordination with the clients' organization to avoid duplication of customer contact
- Utilization of existing dispute management and escalation processes
- Institution of daily activity targets, weekly delinquency goals, and reporting of actual achievement
- Hands-on management of the entire effort

(continues)

CASE STUDY FIVE *(continued)*

The Results

In two months, the results achieved were impressive:

Indicator	Start	Finish	Percent Change
Delinquent A/R*	11.5	6.5	(43)
Percent of total A/R delinquent	52%	35%	(33)
Past due categories :			
1–30 days*	6.7	4.5	(33)
31–60 days*	1.9	0.7	(63)
61–90 days*	1.2	0.1	(92)
> 90 days*	1.7	1.2	(29)
Totals*	11.5	6.5	(43)

*In millions

All actions taken by the dedicated team were thoroughly documented in the client's files, so the client's collection staff could resume activity on the accounts with a minimum of disruption.

CASE STUDY SIX

FOOD PRODUCTS MANUFACTURER

The Company

The company is a $350 million food products manufacturer selling to supermarkets, wholesalers, and mass merchandisers. It had outsourced the invoice to cash process (including deduction processing), to a leading outsourcer, but were unhappy with the results. A work team was organized to establish an in-house capability for this function.

The Solution

Given the urgency of the client's need and the unavailability of the ultimate location for this function, it was moved in-house in two stages:

First, an interim staff, managed and augmented by temporary resources, was assembled in the headquarters location to perform the function

Second, once their southeast U.S. facility was finished and an organization recruited and trained, the function was transferred to the new location

The work team's approach was to:

- Design and document the invoice to cash and deduction processes and workflows
- Optimize the functionality of the existing ERP system (J.D. Edwards)

(continues)

- Design an organization structure, defining number and skill set of staff, reporting relationships, and primary roles and responsibilities

- Design metrics and reporting tailored to their specific needs

- Recruit, augment, and manage the department in its temporary and ultimate location

The Results

The in-house capability was up and running in its ultimate location in seven months. Invoices over 90 days past due were reduced by 70%, open deductions were reduced from $33 million to less than $8 million, and DSO decreased from 43 to 33.

► INDEX